SECOND EDITION

NEW PASSWORD 1
A READING AND VOCABULARY TEXT

Linda Butler
Holyoke Community College

PEARSON
Longman

For Suzanne

New Password 1: A Reading and Vocabulary Text

Pearson Education, 10 Bank Street, White Plains, NY 10606

Staff credits: The people who made up the *New Password 1* team, representing editorial, production, design, and manufacturing, are: Pietro Alongi, Rhea Banker, Dave Dickey, Jaime Lieber, Maria Pia Marrella, Amy McCormick, Linda Moser, Carlos Rountree, Jennifer Stem, and Paula Van Ells.

Development editor: Thomas Ormond
Project editor: Helen B. Ambrosio
Text design & composition: ElectraGraphics, Inc.
Cover design: Maria Pia Marrella
Cover photos: Shutterstock
Illustrations: Len Shalansky and Susan Tait Porcaro

Text credits, photography credits, references, and acknowledgments appear on page 152.

Library of Congress Cataloging-in-Publication Data

Butler, Linda,
     New password 1 : a reading and vocabulary text / Linda Butler.
          p. cm.
     Includes index.
     ISBN-13: 978-0-13-246300-3 (pbk.)
     ISBN-10: 0-13-246300-8 (pbk.)
     ISBN-13: 978-0-13-814343-5 (pbk. with cd)
     ISBN-10: 0-13-814343-9 (pbk. with cd)

1. English language—Textbooks for foreign speakers. 2. Reading comprehension—Problems, exercises, etc. 3. Vocabulary—Problems, exercises, etc. 4. Readers. I. Title. II. Title: New password one.
PE1128.B86137 2009
428.2'4—dc22

2009017284

PEARSON LONGMAN ON THE WEB

Pearsonlongman.com offers online resources for teachers and students. Access our Companion Websites, our online catalog, and our local offices around the world.

Visit us at **pearsonlongman.com**.

Printed in the United States of America
ISBN-13: 978-0-13-246300-3   4   16
ISBN-13: 978-0-13-814343-5   9   16

CONTENTS

SCOPE AND SEQUENCE

Unit/Chapter	Developing Reading Skills	Developing Other Language Skills	Target Vocabulary	
UNIT 1: Learning Something New				
Chapter 1: **Mayda Learns to Swim**	• Identifying the topic and main idea • Remembering details • Summarizing	• Discussing the reading • Using new words • Dictation • Writing sentences about yourself	*afraid* *because* *beginner* *every*	*extra* *learn* *practice* *ready*
Chapter 2: **Learning to Make Movies**	• Identifying the topic and main idea • Remembering details • Summarizing	• Discussing the reading • Using new words • Dictation • Writing sentences with *favorite*	*busy* *everything* *favorite* *just*	*more* *other* *too* *use*
Chapter 3: **Finding Time for Everything**	• Identifying the topic and main idea • Scanning • Summarizing	• Discussing the reading • Using new words • Dictation • Writing sentences with *I have to* and *I like to*	*a few* *early* *enough* *for example*	*have to* *spend* *tired* *well*
UNIT 1 Wrap-up	• Expanding Vocabulary: *everybody, everyone, everywhere* • Extra Reading: *Learning to Drive*, with a review of unit reading skills			
UNIT 2: I'm Hungry! Are You?				
Chapter 4: **The Job of a Food Critic**	• Identifying the topic and main idea • Remembering details • Summarizing	• Discussing the reading • Using new words • Dictation • Writing sentences about a restaurant	*also* *detail* *kind* *maybe*	*most* *smell* *the same* *would like*
Chapter 5: **Who Likes Cereal?**	• Identifying the topic; main idea vs. details • Remembering details • Summarizing	• Discussing the reading • Using new words • Dictation • Writing about your favorite meal of the day	*bowl* *box* *breakfast* *lunch*	*may* *meal* *quick* *snack*
Chapter 6: **The Food Pyramid**	• Identifying the topic; main idea vs. details • Scanning • Summarizing	• Discussing the reading • Using new words • Dictation • Writing about food with *I like* and *I do not like*	*different* *group* *grow* *mean*	*plan* *really* *show* *size*
UNIT 2 Wrap-up	• Expanding Vocabulary: The suffix *-er* (verb + *-er* -> noun) • Extra Reading: *Popcorn*, with a review of unit reading skills			
UNIT 3: Having Fun				
Chapter 7: **An Easy Game**	• Identifying the topic and main idea • Scanning • Diagramming ideas from the reading	• Discussing the reading • Using new words • Dictation • Writing sentences about games	*around* *beat* *both* *each*	*hold* *rule* *try* *world*
Chapter 8: **A New and Different Sport**	• Identifying the topic and main idea • Giving details • Summarizing • Using a graphic organizer	• Discussing the reading • Using new words • Dictation • Writing sentences about sports	*agree* *catch* *enjoy* *field*	*happen* *problem* *seem* *team*

Unit/Chapter	Developing Reading Skills	Developing Other Language Skills	Target Vocabulary	
Chapter 9: Collectors	• Identifying the topic and main idea • Finding examples • Giving details • Using a graphic organizer	• Discussing the reading • Using new words • Dictation • Writing sentences about you and your friends	carry collect hope laugh	pick up remember together without
UNIT 3 Wrap-up	• Expanding Vocabulary: Nouns • Extra Reading: *Do You Like Puzzles?*, with a review of unit reading skills			
UNIT 4: Shopping				
Chapter 10: Mystery Shoppers	• Identifying the topic and main idea • Reading for details • What the reading does and doesn't say • Summarizing • Using a graphic organizer	• Discussing the reading • Using new words • Writing a short paragraph about shopping	almost get rich keep nothing often	own report salesperson so understand
Chapter 11: Online Shoppers	• Identifying the topic and main idea • Reading for details • What the reading does and doesn't say • Summarizing	• Discussing the reading • Using new words • Writing a short paragraph about online shopping	anything decide expensive hard information	price safe usually wear worry
Chapter 12: Returns and Exchanges	• Identifying the topic and main idea • Reading for details • What the reading does and doesn't say • Summarizing	• Discussing the reading • Using new words • Writing a short paragraph about something you're planning to buy	date fit if leave lose	mistake only return too wrong
UNIT 4 Wrap-up	• Expanding Vocabulary: Verbs • Extra Reading: *Gift Cards*, a review of unit reading skills			
UNIT 5: On the Job				
Chapter 13: Working Teens	• Identifying the topic and expressing the main idea • Scanning • Recognizing fact vs. opinion	• Discussing the reading • Using new words • Writing a short paragraph about high school students working	between during fact half let's	life opinion parent reason should
Chapter 14: Night Work	• Identifying the topic and expressing the main idea • Reading for details • Recognizing fact vs. opinion • Using a graphic organizer	• Discussing the reading • Using new words • Writing a short paragraph about yourself: morning person or night owl?	accident body company difficult forget	get hurt hard machine shift stress
Chapter 15: Working for Tips	• Identifying the topic and expressing the main idea • Reading for details • Summarizing	• Discussing the reading • Using new words • Writing a short paragraph about tipping	angry believe bill change expect	fair future large over soon
UNIT 5 Wrap-up	• Expanding Vocabulary: Adjectives • Extra Reading: *Help for Working Parents*, with a review of unit reading skills			

THE SECOND EDITION OF THE *PASSWORD* SERIES

Welcome to *New Password*, the second edition of *Password*, a series designed to help learners of English develop their reading skills and expand their vocabularies. The series offers theme-based units consisting of:

- engaging nonfiction reading passages,
- a variety of skill-development activities based on the passages, and
- exercises to help students understand, remember, and use new words.

With this new edition, the *Password* series expands from three levels to five. Each book can be used independently of the others, but when used as a series, the books will help students reach the 2,000-word vocabulary level in English, at which point, research has shown, most learners can begin to read unadapted texts.

The series is based on two central ideas. The first is that the best way for learners to develop their ability to read English is, as you might guess, to practice reading English. To spark and sustain the student's motivation to read, "second language reading instruction must find ways to avoid continually frustrating the reader."[1] Learners need satisfying reading materials at an appropriate level of difficulty, materials that do not make them feel as if they are struggling to decipher a puzzle.

The level of difficulty is determined by many factors, but one key factor is the familiarity of the vocabulary. Note that

> There is now a large body of studies indicating that poor readers primarily differ from good readers in context-free word recognition, and not in deficiencies in ability to use context to form predictions.[2]

To be successful, readers must be able to recognize a great many words quickly. So in addition to providing engaging reading matter, the *Password* series carefully controls and recycles the vocabulary.

The second idea underlying the design of the series is that textbooks should teach the vocabulary that will be most useful to learners. Corpus-based research has shown that the 2,000 highest-frequency words in English account for almost 80 percent of the running words in academic texts.[3] These are thus highly valuable words for students to learn, and these are the words targeted in the *Password* series.

The chart below shows the number of words that each *New Password* book assumes will be familiar to the learner and the range of the high-frequency vocabulary targeted in the book. Target word choices are based on analyses

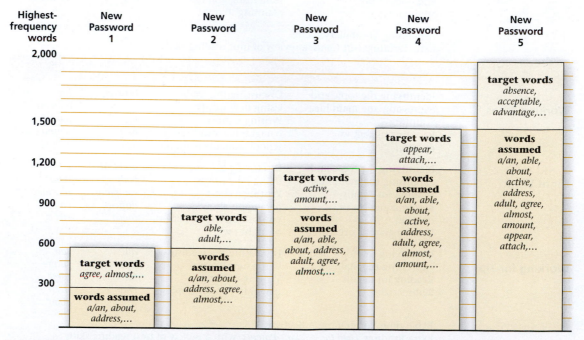

Highest-frequency words	New Password 1	New Password 2	New Password 3	New Password 4	New Password 5
2,000					**target words** *absence, acceptable, advantage,…*
1,500				**target words** *appear, attach,…*	**words assumed** *a/an, able, about, active, address, adult, agree, almost, amount, appear, attach,…*
1,200			**target words** *active, amount,…*	**words assumed** *a/an, able, about, active, address, adult, agree, almost, amount,…*	
900		**target words** *able, adult,…*	**words assumed** *a/an, able, about, address, adult, agree, almost,…*		
600	**target words** *agree, almost,…*	**words assumed** *a/an, about, address, agree, almost,…*			
300	**words assumed** *a/an, about, address,…*				

[1]Thom Hudson, *Teaching Second Language Reading* (Oxford, UK: Oxford University Press, 2007) 291.
[2]C. Juel, quoted in *Teaching and Researching Reading*, William Grabe and Fredericka Stoller (Harlow, England: Pearson Education, 2002) 73.
[3]I. S. P. Nation, *Learning Vocabulary in Another Language* (Cambridge, England: Cambridge University Press, 2001) 17.

of authentic language data in various corpora, including data in the Longman Corpus Network, to determine which words are most frequently used and most likely to be needed by the learner. Also targeted are common collocations and other multiword units, such as phrasal verbs.[4] The target vocabulary is chosen most often for its usefulness across a range of subjects but occasionally for its value in dealing with the topic of one particular chapter. Other factors include the complexity of a word's meanings and uses.

While becoming a good reader in English involves much more than knowing the meanings of words, there is no doubt that vocabulary knowledge is essential. To learn new words, students need to see them repeatedly and in varied contexts. They must become skilled at guessing meaning from context but can do this successfully only when they understand the context. Research by Paul Nation and Liu Na suggests that "for successful guessing [of unknown words] . . . at least 95% of the words in the text must be familiar to the reader."[5] For that reason, the vocabulary in the readings has been carefully controlled so that unknown words should constitute no more than five percent of the text.

The words used in a reading are limited to those high-frequency words that the learner is assumed to know plus the vocabulary targeted in the chapter and target words recycled from previous chapters. New vocabulary is explained and practiced, encountered again in later chapters, and reviewed in the Unit Wrap-ups and Self-Tests. This emphasis on systematic vocabulary acquisition is a highlight of the *Password* series.

The second edition has expanded the series from three levels to five, increasing the number of reading passages from 76 to 104 and expanding the coverage of high-frequency vocabulary. One completely new book has joined the series, *New Password 1. New Password 2, 3, 4,* and *5* have retained the most popular materials from the first edition and added new chapters. The books vary somewhat in organization and content, to meet the diverse needs of beginning- to high-intermediate-level students, but all five feature the popular Unit Wrap-ups and Vocabulary Self-Tests, and all five will help learners make steady progress in developing their English language skills.

Linda Butler, creator of the Password *series*

OVERVIEW OF *NEW PASSWORD 1*

New Password 1 is intended for beginning-level students who know approximately 300 English words. To help these beginners build a solid foundation in English, most of the target vocabulary for each chapter comes from among the 600 highest-frequency words in English. The new vocabulary is introduced in the reading passage for one chapter, practiced in that chapter, and later recycled, with the result that students encounter each target word or phrase at least ten times. Because of the systematic building of vocabulary, as well as the progression of reading skills taught, it is best to do the chapters in order.

Organization of the Book

New Password 1 contains five units, each with three chapters followed by a Wrap-up chapter. After Units 2, 4, and 5, there are Vocabulary Self-Tests. At the end of the book, you will find the Vocabulary Self-Tests Answer Key and an index to the target vocabulary.

THE UNITS Each unit is based on a theme. Each chapter in the unit offers a reading that relates to that theme and focuses on real people, places, events, and ideas.

THE CHAPTERS Each chapter is organized into four sections as follows:

Getting Ready to Read—The chapter opens with a photo and pre-reading questions for class discussion. Students get ready for the reading by examining the photo, discussing what they already know or believe about the topic, and meeting some new vocabulary. A *Read to Find Out* question, which the reading passage will answer, helps students anticipate the content of the reading.

Reading—The reading passages in *New Password 1* progress from about 175 to about 250 words and also progress in their level of reading difficulty (as determined by sentence length, grammar, and syntax as well as vocabulary). Students should do the reading the first time without dictionaries; for this reason, you may wish to have them do their first reading in class. Make sure students understand that multiple readings are essential to improve their comprehension and reading

---

[4]Dilin Liu, "The Most Frequently Used Spoken American English Idioms: A Corpus Analysis and Its Implications," *TESOL Quarterly* 37 (Winter 2003): 4, 671-700.
[5]Nation 254

fluency. Students can reread the passages on their own, and/or as you read aloud, and/or while listening to the audio recording (available on CD). Listening while reading can help students' comprehension, retention of information, and awareness of stress and pronunciation. Reading aloud by students, if desired, can be done in pairs or with the full class once they are quite familiar with the reading passage.

Each reading is followed by a *Quick Comprehension Check,* which includes a brief true/false exercise that lets students check their general understanding. It is a good idea to go over these statements in class. When students tell you a statement is true, ask how they know it is true; when it is false, ask them to correct it. By doing so, you send students back into the reading to find support for their answers. The *Quick Comprehension Check* also follows up on the "Read to Find Out" question from *Getting Ready to Read.* Ask students to give you those answers that are simple and straightforward, but with the more challenging questions (such as "How do you play the game Rock, Paper, Scissors?"), ask students only whether they think they know the answer. Have them actually give it later, when you get to *Discussing the Reading.* During this brief *Quick Comprehension Check* discussion, stick to the main points of the reading and try to avoid spending time explaining vocabulary.

Exploring Vocabulary—Once students have a basic understanding of the reading, it is time to focus on the target vocabulary. Note that many high-frequency words have multiple meanings and function as more than one part of speech, but each target word, as used in the reading and practiced in the exercises, is used as one part of speech with a single meaning. Students may ask about other uses of target words, and of course you will want to answer their questions. However, avoid overwhelming them with more information than they can absorb.

Exploring Vocabulary helps provide the multiple encounters with new words that students need to understand and remember them. In Chapter 1, Exercise A gives a list of the target words, in alphabetical order; in every other chapter, the student must create the list. Exercise B restates ideas from the reading with explanations of the target words in the order they appeared in the reading. Exercise C uses illustrations to explain the remaining target words. Additional exercises give students the chance to work with the vocabulary in new contexts. If after working through all the exercises, students want further information about word meanings, they can turn to their dictionaries. For students at this level, a bilingual dictionary is most appropriate.

Developing Your Skills—In this section are tasks that turn students' focus back on the reading. First, the learner is asked to re-read and then identify the topic and main idea of each reading. The exercises that follow focus on scanning, finding examples or other details in the reading, completing summaries, using graphic organizers, and recognizing fact versus opinion. These exercises prepare students for the questions under *Discussing the Reading.* Your students may be able to discuss them in pairs or small groups, followed by a full-class discussion, or they may need you to guide all discussions with the whole class together. The discussion is intended to reinforce students' understanding of the reading, get them to speak about it, let them make connections between the reading and their own experiences, and elicit their opinions. The next section, *Using New Words,* is about using the target vocabulary in writing. By completing sentences, students can demonstrate their understanding of new words while using them creatively and accurately. Finally, in *Writing,* students complete the chapter with simple writing tasks: a dictation and writing a few sentences (in Chapters 1–9) or writing a simple paragraph (in Chapters 10–15).

THE UNIT WRAP-UPS Each unit ends in a four-part *Unit Wrap-up.* The *Wrap-up* provides a review of the target vocabulary for the unit (in a multiple-choice exercise and a crossword puzzle) and introduces related words or word grammar. It ends with a new reading passage that relates to the unit theme and recycles target vocabulary. The reading is followed by the same types of comprehension and reading skill exercises that the students did in the unit and that appear on the test for that unit.

THE VOCABULARY SELF-TESTS Three multiple-choice *Vocabulary Self-Tests* appear in the book, the first covering target vocabulary from Units 1 and 2, the second covering Units 3 and 4, and the third covering all five units. The answers can be found on page 00.

INDEX TO TARGET VOCABULARY The text ends with an alphabetized list of the target vocabulary.

THE AUDIO PROGRAM Audio recordings of the reading passage and list of target vocabulary for each chapter are available on audio CD.

THE TEACHER'S MANUAL The Teacher's Manual for *New Password 1* contains: Teaching tips and suggested activities for each chapter, the answer key for all exercises in the book, and five unit tests with answers.

UNIT

1

LEARNING SOMETHING NEW

Mayda Learns to Swim

*Mayda in the pool
at school*

GETTING READY TO READ

Talk about these questions with your class.

1. Look at the photo of Mayda in the pool. How old is she?
2. Do students in your country learn to swim at school?
3. Are these good places to swim? Circle *Yes* or *No*. Tell why or why not.

In a lake?
Yes / No

In a river?
Yes / No

In the ocean?
Yes / No

READ TO FIND OUT: Does Mayda swim in the ocean?

READING

Look at the words and picture next to the reading. Then read. Do not stop to use a dictionary.

Mayda Learns to Swim

1   Mayda Saldana is from Mexico. Now she is a college student in the United States. **Every** day, she goes to her classes. For one class, she does not have papers or books. This class is not in a classroom. It is in a pool. It is a swimming class.

2   Mayda's class is for **beginners**. Swimming is new for them. Mayda is **afraid** of the water. The class is not easy for her. She says, "It's easy for children to **learn** new things. But I'm not young!"

3   Mayda's sister can swim, and Mayda's friends can swim. She wants to go swimming with them. She does not like feeling afraid. She goes to class **because** she wants to learn. She **practices** swimming in class. She gets **extra** time in the pool on weekends.

4   Now Mayda says, "I'm not very good, but I'm learning, little by little.[1] The pool is OK now. I'm not afraid of the pool. But the ocean? Oh no, I'm not **ready** for that. There are things like sharks[2] in the ocean!"

[1] *little by little =*
   slowly

[2] *a shark*

Quick Comprehension Check

 Read these sentences about the reading. Circle T (true) or F (false).

1. Mayda goes to college in the United States. (T) F

2. One of her classes is in a swimming pool. T F

3. The class is easy for Mayda. T F

4. She feels OK in the pool now. T F

5. She loves to swim in the ocean. T F

B   Can you answer the Read to Find Out question on page 2?

EXPLORING VOCABULARY

A   These words come from "Mayda Learns to Swim" on page 3. They are in **alphabetical order**.

1. afraid
2. because
3. beginners
4. every

5. extra
6. learn
7. practices
8. ready

B   Complete the sentences with the words in the box. The sentences are about the reading.

because	beginners	✔ every	extra	learn

1. Mayda has classes on Monday, Tuesday, Wednesday, Thursday, and Friday. She goes to class _____every_____ day of the week.

2. Swimming is new for the students in Mayda's class. This is their first time in a swimming class. They are _____.

3. Mayda goes to school to _____ new things. Her teachers help her do this.

4. Why does Mayda go to swimming class? She goes _____ she wants to learn to swim.

5. Mayda swims in class, but the classes are short. She goes to the pool on weekends because she wants _____ time to practice.

C Complete the sentences about the pictures. Write *afraid, practicing,* or *ready.*

1. She is _____ . **2.** She is _____ . **3.** He is _____ to run.

D Complete the sentences with the words in the box.

beginner	every	practices	ready

1. Ann goes to bed at 11:00 _____ night.

2. Paolo is starting to study English. English is new for him. He is a

_____ .

3. It is time to go to school. I have my books. I am _____ to go.

4. Tina is a basketball player. She _____ from 3:00 to 5:00 P.M. every day.

E Complete the sentences with the words in the box.

afraid	because	extra	learn

1. Robert is not going to class today _____ he feels sick.

2. There are 10 people but 12 chairs. There are two _____ chairs.

3. Some people are _____ of flying. They do not like airplanes.

4. Many babies _____ to walk when they are one year old.

DEVELOPING YOUR SKILLS

The Topic and the Main Idea

A Go back to page 3 and read "Mayda Learns to Swim" again.

B Answer the questions about the topic and the main idea of the reading.

> A reading has a **topic**. Ask, "What is the reading about?" The answer is the topic.

1. What is the topic of the reading on page 3? Check (✓) your answer.
   - ☐ **a.** College classes
   - ☐ **b.** Mayda Saldana
   - ☐ **c.** Things in the ocean

> A reading has a **main idea**. Ask, "What does the reading say about the topic?" The answer is the main idea.

2. What is the main idea of the reading? Check (✓) your answer.
   - ☐ **a.** You can learn to swim at school.
   - ☐ **b.** Some people are afraid of the water.
   - ☐ **c.** Mayda Saldana is learning to swim in college.

> The **title** of this reading is "Mayda Learns to Swim." Sometimes the title of a reading tells you the topic. Sometimes the title tells you the main idea.

Remembering Details

Which sentence is true? Circle *a* or *b*.

1. **a.** Mayda Saldana goes to college in Mexico.
   b. Mayda Saldana goes to college in the United States.
2. **a.** Mayda is afraid of the water.
   b. Mayda is afraid of her swimming teacher.
3. **a.** Mayda says, "It's easy for me to learn new things."
   b. Mayda says, "It's easy for children to learn new things."
4. **a.** Her sisters and brothers can swim.
   b. Her sister and her friends can swim.
5. **a.** Mayda says, "The pool is OK now."
   b. Mayda says, "The ocean is OK now."

Summarizing the Reading

A **summary** of a reading is short. It tells the important things about the reading.

Complete the summary of the reading on page 3. Write *afraid, beginners, learning,* or *practices*.

Mayda Saldana is _____learning_____ to swim in college. She is in a
                          (1)

swimming class for _____. She is _____ of the
                    (2)   (3)

water, but that does not stop her. She _____ in class and on
                                                 (4)

weekends.

Discussing the Reading

Talk about these questions with your class.

1. Why does Mayda want to learn to swim?
2. Mayda says, "It's easy for children to learn new things. But I'm not young!" What do you think: Is it easy for children to learn new things? Is it easy for them to learn English? Tell why or why not.
3. Mayda is afraid of the water, but she goes in the pool. Is it good to do things that you are afraid of?
4. Mayda practices swimming on weekends. Do you practice English on weekends? Tell why or why not.

Using New Words

Work alone or with a partner. Complete the sentences. Write your sentences on a piece of paper.

1. Our class **begins** at _____ : _____ (A.M. / P.M.)
2. Many people are **afraid** of _____.
3. I need to **practice** _____.
4. I want to learn English **because** _____.
5. I _____ **every** day.

Writing

A Get ready for a **dictation**. (You will listen and write.) Practice writing these sentences.

1. Go to school.
2. Be ready to learn.
3. Work with your class.
4. Don't be afraid.
5. Find extra time to practice English.

Close your book. Take a piece of paper. Your teacher will say the sentences. Listen and write the sentences.

B Read the questions. Complete the answers.

1. What is your name?

   My name is _____.
2. Where are you from?

   I am from _____.
3. Where do you go to school?

   I am a student at _____.
4. What are you learning?

   I am learning _____.

C Copy your sentences from B.1–4 on a piece of paper.

Learning to Make Movies

Will Daniel with a video camera

GETTING READY TO READ

Talk about these questions with your class.

1. Look at the photo. What do you see?

2. What are the names of these actors? Who are some actors that you like?

3. How many people in the class watch movies on DVDs?

4. Do you, your family, or your friends make movies? Tell when and how.

> **READ TO FIND OUT:** What does Will do in the summer?

READING

Look at the words and picture next to the reading. Then read. Do not stop to use a dictionary.

Learning to Make Movies

1   Will Daniel loves movies. He and his friends like to go see new movies. But Will does not **just** watch movies. He is learning to make movies, **too**. He is learning at home, at his high school, and at film[1] school. Read this interview[2] with Will.

2   *Interviewer:*   Will, how are you learning about making movies?

3   *Will:*   At home, I watch movies on DVDs. Sometimes a DVD has an interview with the director.[3] You can learn a lot by listening to directors.

4   *Interviewer:*   Do you have a **favorite** director?

5   *Will:*   Yeah, Steven Spielberg. He makes great movies.

6   *Interviewer:*   What about in school? Can you learn about moviemaking at your high school?

7   *Will:*   I'm taking an acting class. And I'm learning to **use** a movie camera.[4] Sometimes I make movies with the **other** people in the class. We make short movies, just four or five minutes long.

8   *Interviewer:*   And you go to film school in the summer, don't you?

9   *Will:*   That's right. I learn about acting and directing there, too. We do a little of **everything**—writing, making costumes,[5] using lights. We're **busy** from morning to night, with classes eight or nine hours a day, and sometimes **more**.

10   *Interviewer:*   That's a lot of work! What about after high school? Do you want to study film in college?

11   *Will:*   I want to study acting, but my mom and dad don't like that idea.

[1] *film* = movie

[2] an *interview* = a conversation with one person asking many questions

[3] a *director* = the person who tells the actors in a movie what to do

[4] a *movie camera*

[5] *costumes* = clothes for actors

Quick Comprehension Check

A Read these sentences about the reading. Circle T (true) or F (false).

1. Will is learning to make movies.   (T)   F

2. He watches movies on DVDs.   T   F

3. He is a college student.   T   F

4. He is taking acting and singing classes.   T   F

5. He goes to film school in the summer.   T   F

B Can you answer the Read to Find Out question on page 9?

EXPLORING VOCABULARY

A Find the words in **bold** in "Learning to Make Movies" on page 10. Write them in the list. Use alphabetical order.

1. busy   5. _____

2. everything   6. _____

3. _____   7. _____

4. _____   8. _____

B Complete the sentences with the words in the box. The sentences are about the reading.

busy	everything	✔ just	more	too

1. Many people watch movies and don't think about them much. But Will doesn't _____just_____ watch movies. He studies them.

2. Will watches movies, and he makes movies, _____.

3. At film school, Will learns all about making movies. He wants to know _____ about making movies.

4. Will has many, many things to do at film school. He is _____ all day.

5. Sometimes Will is in class for _____ than nine hours. He is there for 10 hours or 11 hours or . . .

C Complete the sentences about the picture. Write *favorite*, *other*, or *using*.

The woman on the left is _____using_____ a TV camera.
(1)

The _____ woman
(2)
has a microphone. She is doing an interview with the man. He is an actor. Many people like him. He is their _____ actor.
(3)

D Complete the sentences with the words in the box.

busy	favorite	just	other

1. Maria is a student and a mother. She has a job, too. She is a _____ woman.

2. I love weekends. Saturday and Sunday are my _____ days of the week.

3. Max does not talk in class. He _____ listens.

4. Lucy likes cats, just cats. She does not like _____ animals.

E Complete the conversations with the words in the box.

everything	more	too	use

1. **A:** Can I please _____ your phone?
   B: OK. Here you go.

2. **A:** Why do you want a new job?
   B: I need _____ money.

3. **A:** Do you have your books? A pen? A pencil? Some paper?
   B: Yes, I have _____ in my bag. I'm ready to go.

4. **A:** Will Smith is my favorite actor.
   B: I like him, _____.

DEVELOPING YOUR SKILLS

The Topic and the Main Idea

A Go back to page 10 and read "Learning to Make Movies" again.

B Answer the questions about the topic and the main idea of the reading.

> Remember:
>
> What is the **topic**? = What is the reading about?
>
> What is the **main idea**? = What does the reading say about the topic?

1. What is the topic of the reading on page 10? Check (✓) your answer.
   - ☐ **a.** Actors and directors
   - ☐ **b.** Film school
   - ☐ **c.** Will Daniel
2. What is the main idea of the reading? Check (✓) your answer.
   - ☐ **a.** Movies are fun to watch.
   - ☐ **b.** Will Daniel and his friends like to go to the movies.
   - ☐ **c.** Will Daniel is learning about making movies at home and in school.

Remembering Details

Which answer is correct? Circle *a* or *b*.

1. Will goes to see new movies with his _____.
   - **a.** family   **b.** friends
2. Will watches interviews with directors on _____.
   - **a.** DVDs   **b.** TV
3. Steven Spielberg is Will's favorite _____.
   - **a.** actor   **b.** director
4. Will makes movies that are four or five _____ long.
   - **a.** minutes   **b.** hours

5. Will goes to _____ in the summer.
  a. high school   **b.** film school

6. At film school, Will learns about acting, directing, and _____ for movies.
  a. paying   **b.** writing

7. At film school, the students are in class _____ hours a day.
  a. four or five   **b.** eight or more

8. Will wants to study acting in _____.
  a. Hollywood   **b.** college

Summarizing the Reading

Complete the summary of the reading on page 10. Use _acting_, _everything_, _film_, _home_, and _movies_.

Will Daniel loves _____movies_____. He is learning to make them.
                          (1)

He watches interviews with directors on DVDs at _____.
                                                        (2)

At his high school, he takes an _____ class. He goes
                                      (3)

to _____ school in the summer. Will wants to know
      (4)

_____ about making movies.
      (5)

Discussing the Reading

Talk about these questions with your class.

1. How is Will learning about moviemaking? Tell three ways.

2. Would you like to go to film school? Tell why or why not.

3. Will says, "My mom and dad don't like that idea." What is he talking about? Why do you think his mother and father feel that way?

4. What do you want to study? How does your family feel about this?

Using New Words

Work alone or with a partner. Complete the sentences. Write your sentences on a piece of paper.

1. English is a language. Two **other** languages are _____ and _____.
2. It is easy to **use** a _____.
3. I like _____, and my friends do, **too**.
4. I have **just** one _____.
5. I think _____ knows **everything** about _____.

Writing

 Get ready for a dictation. Practice writing these sentences.

1. Call a friend.
2. Talk about movies.
3. Talk about other things, too.
4. Watch a DVD.
5. Do you have a camera?

Close your book. Take a piece of paper. Your teacher will say the sentences. Listen and write the sentences.

B **On a piece of paper, write five sentences about your favorite people and your favorite things (actors, singers, foods, sports, cars, places, . . .).**

Examples:

My favorite colors are blue and green.

My favorite month is September.

Finding Time for Everything

Dan with his guitar, his books, and his laundry

GETTING READY TO READ

Talk about these questions with your class.

1. Look at the photo. What does the photo tell you about Dan?

2. How many hours are you in class every week?

   ☐ 1–5 hours   ☐ 6–10 hours   ☐ 11–20 hours   ☐ more than 20 hours

3. What other things do you do every week?

   Things I NEED to Do

   ☐ work at a job
   ☐ study
   ☐ go food shopping
   ☐ other: _____

   Things I LIKE to Do

   ☐ go out with friends
   ☐ listen to music
   ☐ use a computer
   ☐ other: _____

   READ TO FIND OUT: What is Dan learning to do?

READING

Look at the words and pictures next to the reading. Then read. Do not stop to use a dictionary.

Finding Time for Everything

1   Dan Butler is far from home. His family lives in Hong Kong, but he is studying in the United States. This is his first year in college. He is happy to be there, but he is very **tired**. He is not getting **enough** sleep.

2   Dan is not getting enough sleep because he has many things to do. Every day, he goes to classes. After class, he studies for **a few** hours. Then he goes running. On some days, he works as a lifeguard[1] at the college pool. He **has to** find time for other things, too. **For example**, he has to do his laundry.[2]

3   College cannot be all work, all the time! Dan needs time for fun, too. He is meeting many new people, and he likes **spending** time with them.

4   Dan likes music, too. He can play the guitar **well**. He plays the piano and the cello,[3] too. Every night, he makes music with friends. Then they all go to bed late. In the morning, Dan's classes begin **early**. That is why he is tired. "I yawn[4] a lot in class," he says.

5   "I have to study, and I want to have fun," says Dan, "but I need more sleep. What can I do?" Like other college students, he is learning to manage his time,[5] but it is not easy. Dan wants to know, "How can I find time for everything?"

[1] a *lifeguard*

[2] *do his laundry* = wash his clothes

[3] the *piano* and the *cello*

[4] He's *yawning*.

[5] *manage his time* = use his time well

Quick Comprehension Check

A **Read these sentences about the reading. Circle T (true) or F (false).**

1. Dan is living at home with his family.   T (F)

2. He is busy all day.   T F

3. He is getting a lot of sleep.   T F

4. He likes making music with friends.   T F

5. He is learning to manage his time.   T F

B **Can you answer the Read to Find Out question on page 16?**

EXPLORING VOCABULARY

A **Find the words in bold in "Finding Time for Everything" on page 17. Write them in the list. Use alphabetical order.**

1. a few   5. _____

2. early   6. _____

3. _____   7. _____

4. _____   8. _____

B **Complete the sentences with the words in the box. The sentences are about the reading.**

a few	enough	for example	has to	well

1. Dan needs more sleep. He isn't getting _____ sleep. He doesn't feel good.

2. He studies for _____ hours in the afternoon. He studies for three or four hours.

3. Dan needs to go to class, and he needs to study. He _____ do these things.

4. He has to do other things, too. _____, he has to wash his clothes because he needs clean clothes.

5. Dan is a good guitar player. He can play the guitar _____.

C **Complete the sentences about the pictures. Write *early*, *spending*, or *tired*.**

1. She is _____.

2. He is _____ money.

3. It's _____ in the morning.

D **Match the beginning and the end of each sentence.**

1. I am going to bed because ___ I am tired ___.

2. I have $8, but I need $10. I don't have _____.

3. Joe goes to work at 5:30 A.M. His workday begins _____.

4. You're a good singer! You sing very _____.

well
I am tired
enough money
early in the morning

E **Complete the sentences with the words in the box.**

a few	for example	have to	spends

1. I like fruit. _____, I like oranges, bananas, and apples.
2. There are just _____ people in the pool—three or four people.
3. Richard studies after class. He _____ a lot of time on his homework.
4. Children don't want to get shots, but they _____ get them.

DEVELOPING YOUR SKILLS

The Topic and the Main Idea

A **Go back to page 17 and read "Finding Time for Everything" again.**

B **Answer the questions about the topic and the main idea of the reading.**

1. What is the topic of the reading? Check (✓) your answer.
   - ☐ **a.** College students
   - ☐ **b.** Dan Butler at college
   - ☐ **c.** Finding time for fun
2. What is the main idea of the reading? Check (✓) your answer.
   - ☐ **a.** Dan Butler is learning to find time for everything at college.
   - ☐ **b.** Dan Butler is tired because he has early morning classes.
   - ☐ **c.** College students have many things to do.

Scanning the Reading

When you **scan** a reading, you read it fast to find a word or a number.

Scan the reading on page 17. Find the words to complete the sentences.

1. Dan's family is in _____, but he is in _____.
2. Every day after class, Dan _____ for a few hours.
3. Then he goes _____.
4. Sometimes he works as a _____ at the college pool.
5. Dan likes music. He can play the _____, the _____, and the _____.
6. At night, he plays music with friends and goes to bed _____.
7. He is learning to manage his _____.

Summarizing the Reading

A **Match the beginning and the end of each sentence.**

_c_ 1. Dan Butler is

____ 2. He does not get enough sleep

____ 3. He needs time for

____ 4. For example, he likes

____ 5. He is learning

a. because he has to go to class, study, and work.

b. to make music with friends.

c. a tired college student.

d. to use his time well.

e. fun, too.

B **Copy the sentences to complete the summary.**

Dan Butler is a tired college student. He does not get enough sleep

Discussing the Reading

Talk about these questions with your class.

1. Dan does some things because he has to. What are some examples from the reading?

2. Dan does other things because he likes to. What are some examples from the reading?

3. Dan asks, "How can I find time for everything?" What do you think? What can he do?

4. Dan isn't getting enough sleep. What about you? Tell why or why not.

Using New Words

Work alone or with a partner. Complete the sentences. Write your sentences on a piece of paper.

1. Every day, I **have to** _____.

2. A teacher **has to** _____.

3. Some people don't like to _____ **early** in the morning.

4. Some TV shows are good. **For example**, I like _____
   _____.

5. I like to **spend** time with _____.

Writing

 Get ready for a dictation. Practice writing these sentences.

1. Spend time with your friends.

2. Find time to study, too.

3. Use your time well.

4. Do you get enough sleep?

5. Do you go to bed early?

Close your book. Take a piece of paper. Your teacher will say the sentences. Listen and write the sentences.

B **On a piece of paper, write about your weekends. Complete these sentences.**

1. On weekends, I have to _____. I have to _____, too.

2. On weekends, I like to _____. I like to _____, too.

Examples:

1. On weekends, I have to go to work. I have to do homework, too.

2. On weekends, I like to talk to my sister on the phone. I like to go shopping, too.

Wrap-up

REVIEWING VOCABULARY

Circle the correct word to complete the sentence.

1. Sarah likes cats, but she is _____ of dogs.
   a. beginner   **b.** ready   **c.** afraid

2. Do you have _____ money, or do you need more?
   a. practice   **b.** enough   **c.** favorite

3. Can you _____ a camera?
   a. use   **b.** tired   **c.** spend

4. I don't want to go out _____ it's very cold.
   a. example   **b.** because   **c.** too

5. Please don't eat all the cookies! Take _____ a few.
   a. more   **b.** extra   **c.** just

6. I can't talk on the phone right now. I'm _____.
   a. other   **b.** busy   **c.** early

7. Jack doesn't want to work, but he _____ to. He needs the money.
   a. well   **b.** learn   **c.** has

EXPANDING VOCABULARY

Every

In Chapter 1, you learned the word *every*. In Chapter 2, you learned *everything*. Some other words begin with *every-*. Study these words.

everybody, everyone = all the people

everywhere = in all the places

Complete the sentences. Use *every*, *everything*, *everybody*, *everyone*, and *everywhere*.

1. The students are ready to begin. _____ is in the classroom.
2. I know a little about baseball. I don't know _____.
3. She washes her hair _____ morning before school.
4. There are flowers _____ in her house.
5. Does _____ speak English in the United States?

A PUZZLE

Complete these sentences and the puzzle on page 26. Look at the word lists on pages 4, 11, and 18 for help.

Across

5. We need two cups of sugar to make the cookies. Do we have e_____ sugar?
6. I can't s_____ much money because I don't have much money.
8. There are four people and six chairs. We have two e_____ chairs.
12. Tina loves Italian food. For e_____, she loves pizza.

Down

1. I like the Boston Red Sox. Who is your favorite_____ baseball team?
2. He is starting to learn Spanish. He is a b_____.
3. I can write with just one hand. I can't write with my o_____ hand.
4. We're waiting for Katya. She isn't r_____ to go.

Down (*continued*)

7. To speak English well, you need
   to p_____.

9. I like coffee, and I like tea,
   t_____.

10. Six is m_____ than five.

11. She is taking a swimming class.
    She wants to l_____
    to swim.

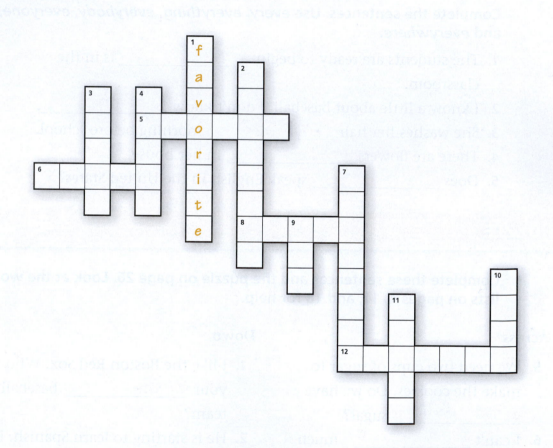

EXTRA READING

Learning to Drive

1   Amina Osman is very happy today. She is beginning something new. She is at her first Driver's Ed class. She is learning about driving a car.

2   "Learning to drive will be a good thing for me," says Amina. Now, she has to get rides from her husband, Ali. But Ali works every day. He does not always have enough time to give her a ride.

3   Sometimes Amina has to take the bus. She is not happy about that because the bus is slow. There is a bus stop near her apartment, but the bus is sometimes late. Amina does not like waiting for it. She does not like standing at the bus stop on cold days, in the rain, or under the hot sun.

4   Amina is happy about learning to drive, but she is a little afraid, too. The cars on the streets of her city go fast. "I'm going to find quiet streets to practice driving," she says. "My husband is going to help me."

5   Ali is listening to Amina. "I'm ready to help my wife," he says, "but I'm a little afraid, too!"

Comprehension Check

Read these sentences about the reading. Circle T (true) or F (false).

1. Amina is happy about learning to drive.   T   F

2. Her husband can drive a car.   T   F

3. Amina always takes the bus.   T   F

4. She likes the bus.   T   F

5. She is afraid of driving on streets with fast cars.   T   F

6. Ali is going to help Amina learn to drive.   T   F

Scanning the Reading

Scan the reading "Learning to Drive." Find the words to complete the sentences.

1. Amina is at her first Driver's Ed _____.

2. Ali is Amina's _____.

3. Amina does not like to take the _____, but sometimes she has to.

4. She does not like waiting at the bus _____.

5. She is a little afraid of driving because other cars go _____.

6. Ali is ready to teach Amina, but he is a little _____.

The Topic and the Main Idea

1. What is the topic of the reading on page 27? Check (✓) your answer.

   ☐ **a.** Buses and cars

   ☐ **b.** Amina Osman

   ☐ **c.** A man and his wife

2. What is the main idea of the reading? Check (✓) your answer.

   ☐ **a.** Amina Osman does not like taking the bus, but sometimes she has to.

   ☐ **b.** Amina Osman is happy about learning to drive, but she is afraid, too.

   ☐ **c.** Amina and her husband, Ali, are learning to drive.

I'M HUNGRY! ARE YOU?

CHAPTER 4

The Job of a Food Critic

Is this woman at work?

GETTING READY TO READ

Talk about these questions with your class.

1. Do you like to:

	Yes	Sometimes	No
talk about food?	☐	☐	☐
read about food?	☐	☐	☐
eat new foods?	☐	☐	☐

2. When do you eat in restaurants?

   ☐ every day   ☐ every week   ☐ every month   ☐ never

3. What kinds of restaurants do you like?

   ☐ Italian restaurants   ☐ fast-food restaurants

   ☐ Chinese restaurants   ☐ seafood restaurants

   ☐ Mexican restaurants   ☐ other: _____

READ TO FIND OUT: What is the job of a food critic?

READING

Look at the words and pictures next to the reading. Then read. Do not stop to use a dictionary.

The Job of a Food Critic

1   Do you love food? **Maybe** you **would like** a job as a food critic. Food critics go to restaurants and write about the food. They write for magazines,[1] newspapers, and websites.[2] The job can be fun, but it is not always easy.

2   First, food critics need to know a lot about food. Some food critics learn by working in restaurant kitchens. Others learn by going to cooking school. All food critics have to read a lot about food.

3   Food critics **also** need to be ready to eat many **kinds** of food. **Most** of the food will taste[3] good, but some will not. Food critics cannot always go to **the same** restaurants and just eat their favorite things. They have to go to new places, and sometimes they have to eat bad food. That part of the job is not fun.

4   Food critics have to be good writers, too. It is not easy to write well about food. Their readers want **details** about the food. For example, how does it look, **smell**, and taste? Their readers want to know about the service,[4] too.

5   Would you like a job as a food critic? Eating and writing about food can be fun, but maybe just eating is more fun.

[1] a *magazine*

[2] a *website* = a page or pages on the Internet

[3] It *tastes* bad.

[4] the *service* = the help that workers in the restaurant give you

Quick Comprehension Check

 A   **Read these sentences about the reading. Circle T (true) or F (false).**

1. A food critic writes about restaurants and their food. **T   F**

2. Food critics work for supermarkets.   **T   F**

3. Food critics have to know a lot about food.   **T   F**

4. Food critics always eat great food.   **T   F**

5. Writing is an important part of a food critic's job.   **T   F**

B   Can you answer the Read to Find Out question on page 30?

EXPLORING VOCABULARY

A   Find the words in **bold** in "The Job of a Food Critic" on page 31. Write them in the list. Use alphabetical order.

1. also _____   5. _____
2. _____   6. _____
3. _____   7. _____
4. _____   8. _____

B   Complete the sentences with the words in the box. The sentences are **about the reading.**

also	details	✔ maybe	most	would like

1. Being a food critic is a good job for some people. _____Maybe_____ it would be a good job for you. I don't know.
2. Maybe you _____ to be a food critic. Do you think it's a good job?
3. Food critics go to great restaurants. They _____ go to bad restaurants.
4. Some of the food they get is bad, but _____ of the food tastes good. Food critics eat more good food than bad food.
5. A food critic's readers want to know: Is the restaurant good or bad? They want to know more, too. They want _____: How does the food look, taste, and smell?

C Complete the sentences about the pictures. Write *kinds*, *the same*, or *smells*.

1. The flower _____ good.

2. Here are five _____ of vegetables.

3. These two birds look _____.

D Complete the sentences with the words in the box.

also	details	most	smells

1. What are you cooking? It _____ great!

2. A few of the students know a lot of English, but _____ of the students are beginners.

3. Greta's first language is German. She can _____ speak French and English.

4. John has a new apartment. I don't know how many rooms there are. I don't know any _____ about the apartment.

E   **Complete the conversations with the words in the box.**

kinds	maybe	the same	would like

1. **A:** Are we going to have a nice weekend?

    B: I don't know. _____ it will rain.

2. **A:** Can I get you something to drink?

    B: Yes, please! I _____ some tea.

3. **A:** What's your favorite fruit?

    B: I don't have a favorite. I like all _____ of fruit.

4. **A:** Do you go to many movies with Lisa?

    B: Yes, I do because we like _____ kind of movies.

DEVELOPING YOUR SKILLS

The Topic and the Main Idea

A   **Go back to page 31 and read "The Job of a Food Critic" again.**

B   **Answer the questions about the topic and the main idea of the reading.**

1. What is the topic of the reading? Check (✓) your answer.
    - ☐ **a.** Food
    - ☐ **b.** Food critics
    - ☐ **c.** Restaurant jobs

2. What is the main idea of the reading? Check (✓) your answer.
    - ☐ **a.** A food critic's job can be fun, but it is not easy.
    - ☐ **b.** Food critics know a lot of good restaurants.
    - ☐ **c.** It is easy to get a job as a food critic.

Remembering Details

Which sentence gives a detail from the reading? Circle *a* or *b*.

1. **a.** Food critics sometimes work for supermarkets.

    b. Food critics sometimes work for newspapers.

2. **a.** Food critics eat in many restaurants.

    b. Food critics cook in many restaurants.

3. **a.** A food critic has to know a lot about food.

   b. A food critic has to make a lot of food.

4. **a.** Some food critics learn by working in restaurant kitchens.

   b. Some food critics learn by working in high school kitchens.

5. **a.** Food critics always get great food.

   b. Food critics sometimes get bad food.

6. **a.** Food critics have to write well.

   b. Food critics have to write fast.

Summarizing the Reading

Complete the summary of the reading on page 31. Use *also*, *easy*, *kinds*, *know*, and *restaurants*.

Food critics eat in _____. Then they write about
₍₁₎

the food for a newspaper, magazine, or website. Food critics have

to _____ a lot about food. They have to eat many
₍₂₎

_____ of food. They _____ have to write well. The
₍₃₎   ₍₄₎

job is not _____, but it can be fun.
₍₅₎

Discussing the Reading

Talk about these questions with your class.

1. How do food critics learn about food? Tell three ways. What other ways can a person learn about food?

2. What do you think: Who pays when a food critic eats in a restaurant?

3. Why do people read what food critics write? Do you ever read what they write?

4. Would you like to be a food critic? Tell why or why not.

Using New Words

Work alone or with a partner. Complete the sentences. Then copy your sentences on a piece of paper.

1. I like many **kinds** of _____.

2. I always use **the same** _____.

3. _____ and _____ **smell** good.

4. **I would like** _____.

5. **Maybe** _____.

Writing

A **Get ready for a dictation. Practice writing these sentences.**

1. Many people love good food.

2. Some people like restaurants.

3. Do you like many kinds of food?

4. Would you like to go out to eat?

Close your book. Take a piece of paper. Your teacher will say the sentences. Listen and write the sentences.

B **Think of a restaurant you like. Answer these questions about it. Write your answers on a piece of paper.**

1. What is the name of the restaurant?

2. Where is it?

3. What kind of food does it have?

4. When do you go there?

Examples:

1. The name of the restaurant is Pintu's.

2. It is in West Springfield.

3. It has Indian food.

4. Sometimes I go on Friday night.

Who Likes Cereal?

His favorite snack

GETTING READY TO READ

Talk about these questions with your class.

1. Look at the photo. What do you see?
2. What kinds of cereal can you name?
3. Do many people in your country eat cereal?
4. Who do you know that eats cereal? Tell when they eat it.

READ TO FIND OUT: Who eats cereal in the United States?

READING

Look at the words next to the reading. Then read. Do not stop to use a dictionary.

Who Likes Cereal?

1   Some people say "**breakfast** cereal." Some say "cold cereal." Most people just say "cereal." They are all talking about the same thing. They are talking about an important food in the United States.

2   You can find cereal in every U.S. supermarket. You **may** find 200 kinds of it! More than 90 percent[1] of Americans say they like cereal. They buy a lot of it. They buy more than two billion[2] **boxes** of cereal a year. They spend a lot of money on it, too. They spend more on cereal than on bread or hamburger.

3   Many people in the United States, young and old, eat cereal every morning, but cereal is not just for breakfast. Children can buy cereal for **lunch** at school. Many college students eat it as a **snack**. They eat it at all hours of the day and night. A few colleges have cereal cafés[3] for their students. At these cafés, cereal is all there is.

4   Some people eat cereal for supper,[4] too. They may be tired when they come home from work. They may not want to take the time to cook. A **bowl** of cereal with milk is a **quick** and easy **meal**. Some people do not wait for the bowl or the milk. They just eat their cereal out of the box.

[1] *percent* = %

[2] *two billion* = 2,000,000,000

[3] a *café* = a small restaurant

[4] *supper* = a meal eaten in the evening

Quick Comprehension Check

(A) **Read these sentences about the reading. Circle T (true) or F (false).**

1. "Breakfast cereal" and "cold cereal" are two names
    for the same thing.   T   F

2. All supermarkets in the United States have cereal.   T   F

3. People in the United States eat cereal just in the
    morning.   T   F

4. A few college students like cereal but not many.   T   F

5. Many people, young and old, eat cereal in the
    United States.   T   F

(B) **Can you answer the Read to Find Out question on page 37?**

EXPLORING VOCABULARY

(A) **Find the words in bold in "Who Likes Cereal?" on page 38. Write them
in the list. Use alphabetical order.**

1. bowl _____   5. _____

2. _____   6. _____

3. _____   7. _____

4. _____   8. _____

(B) **Complete the sentences with the words in the box. The sentences are
about the reading.**

lunch	may	meals	quick	snack

1. At a U.S. supermarket, you _____ find just a few kinds of
    cereal, or maybe there will be 200 kinds!

2. Many children eat breakfast at home before school. Later, they eat
    _____ at school in the late morning or at 12:00 P.M.

3. Sometimes you don't want to eat a lot of food. You want just a small meal or a _____, like a bowl of cereal.

4. You don't need a lot of time for cereal. It's _____ and easy to eat.

5. Some people eat just three times a day. Others eat three _____ and snacks, too.

C Complete the sentences about the picture. Write *bowl*, *box*, or *breakfast*.

The man in the picture is having

_____. There is a
(1)

_____ of fruit on the table. There is
(2)

a _____ of cereal next to the fruit.
(3)

D Match the words and their meanings. Write the letters.

__*b*__ 1. meal

____ 2. breakfast

____ 3. snack

____ 4. lunch

a. the first meal of the day

b. food that you eat at one time

c. a meal eaten in the middle of the day

d. a small amount of food that you eat between meals

E Complete the conversations with the words in the box.

bowl	box	may	quick

1. **A:** What's in this _____?

   B: My new computer.

2. **A:** Will you put some water in the cat's _____?

   B: OK.

3. **A:** Are you going to see your sister?

   B: Yes, but it'll be just a _____ visit—maybe 15 minutes.

4. A: Is it raining?

   B: Not right now, but it _____ rain later.

DEVELOPING YOUR SKILLS

The Topic and the Main Idea

A   Go back to page 38 and read "Who Likes Cereal?" again.

B   Answer the questions about the topic and the main idea of the reading.

1. What is the topic of the reading? Check (✓) your answer.
   - ☐ **a.** Good breakfasts for children
   - ☐ **b.** Favorite foods in the United States
   - ☐ **c.** Cereal in the United States

2. One sentence gives the main idea of the reading. The other three sentences give details from the reading. Write *main idea* or *detail* on the line.

   _____detail_____ **a.** Some U.S. supermarkets have 200 kinds of cereal.

   _____ **b.** Some children get cereal at school for their lunch.

   _____ **c.** Cereal is an important food in the United States.

   _____ **d.** Some people eat their cereal out of the box.

Remembering Details

Which sentence gives a detail from the reading? Circle *a* or *b*.

1. **a.** Cereal, cold cereal, and breakfast cereal are three kinds of food.
   b. *Cereal, cold cereal,* and *breakfast cereal* are three names for the same thing.

2. **a.** You can find cereal in most U.S. supermarkets.
   b. You can find cereal in every U.S. supermarket.

3. **a.** Everyone in the United States eats cereal for breakfast.
   b. Most people in the United States say they like cereal.

4. a. People in the United States buy more than two billion boxes of cereal a year.

   b. People in the United States eat more than two billion bowls of cereal a year.

5. a. They spend more money on cereal than on bread or hamburger.

   b. They spend more money on cereal than on milk.

6. a. Many U.S. college students love cereal for snacks.

   b. Every U.S. college has a cereal café.

7. a. Most people eat cereal out of the box with no milk.

   b. Some people eat cereal out of the box with no milk.

Summarizing the Reading

 A   **Match the beginning and the end of each sentence.**

_c_ **1.** Most people in the United States

_____ **2.** Every U.S. supermarket

_____ **3.** People young and old eat it, and not

_____ **4.** They may eat cereal at

_____ **5.** They like it

a. just for breakfast.

b. for snacks, too.

c. like cereal.

d. has many kinds of it.

e. any meal of the day.

B   **Copy the sentences to complete the summary.**

> Most people in the United States like cereal.
> Every U.S.

Discussing the Reading

Talk about these questions with your class.

1. Who eats cereal in the United States?
2. When and where do people in the United States eat cereal?
3. Is cereal a good breakfast? Is it a good lunch? Is it a good snack? Is it a good supper? Tell why or why not.

Using New Words

Work alone or with a partner. Complete the sentences. Then copy your sentences on a piece of paper.

1. When I want a **snack**, I eat _____ or _____.
2. I eat _____ in a **bowl**.
3. My favorite thing for **lunch** is _____.
4. A **quick** and easy meal for me is _____.
5. **Most** of my friends _____.

Writing

 Get ready for a dictation. Practice writing these sentences.

1. I eat breakfast every day.
2. Do you have lunch at school?
3. I like a snack in the afternoon.
4. What is your favorite meal of the day?

Close your book. Take a piece of paper. Your teacher will say the sentences. Listen and write the sentences.

 Write your answers to these questions on a piece of paper.

1. What is your favorite meal of the day?
2. Where and when do you like to have it?
3. What do you like to eat for this meal?

Examples:

1. My favorite meal of the day is breakfast.
2. I have my breakfast at home at 7:30 A.M.
3. Most days, I have orange juice, coffee, and toast with strawberry jam.

The Food Pyramid

He's hungry!

GETTING READY TO READ

Talk about these questions with your class.

1. Look at the photo. What do you see?
2. Match these words with the pictures: *beans, fruit, grains, meat, milk, oil,* and *vegetables.*

a. b. c. d. e. f. g.

3. Look at the food in the pictures. Which kinds do you eat every day?

READ TO FIND OUT: What is the Food Pyramid?

READING

Look at the picture and the words next to the reading. Then read. Do not stop to use a dictionary.

The Food Pyramid

1   Children have to eat well to **grow**. We all have to eat well to feel good. "Eating well" **means** eating the right kinds of food. It also means eating the right amounts[1] of food. The Food Pyramid is one **plan** for eating well.

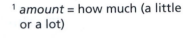
[1] *amount* = how much (a little or a lot)

2   The pyramid has six parts. The six parts are for six food **groups**. From left to right, they are: (1) grains, (2) vegetables, (3) fruit, (4) oil, (5) milk, and (6) meat and beans.

3   There are **different** kinds of food in each group. For example, the milk group includes[2] cheese and yogurt. The meat and beans group includes fish and eggs. The Food Pyramid plan says to eat food from all the groups every day.

[2] *includes* = has something in it as a part

4   The six parts of the pyramid are different **sizes**. For example, the first part, for grains, is big. That means, "Eat a lot of grains." The part for oil is very small. We need some oil, but not a lot.

5   The Food Pyramid does not **show** every kind of food. For example, there is no tea or coffee in the plan. There is also no chocolate.

6   Most people in the United States know about the Food Pyramid. Children study it in school. But do most people **really** eat this way? What do you think?

Quick Comprehension Check

A **Read these sentences about the reading. Circle T (true) or F (false).**

1. The Food Pyramid tells people what is good to eat. T F

2. The Food Pyramid has six parts. T F

3. Meat and milk are in one part. T F

4. The Food Pyramid says to eat more grains than oil. T F

5. The Food Pyramid has every kind of food and drink. T F

B **Can you answer the Read to Find Out question on page 44?**

EXPLORING VOCABULARY

A **Find the words in bold in "The Food Pyramid" on page 45. Write them in the list. Use alphabetical order.**

1. different _____

2. _____

3. _____

4. _____

5. _____

6. _____

7. _____

8. _____

B **Complete the sentences with the words in the box. The sentences are about the reading.**

group	mean	plan	really	size

1. Some people have questions about "eating well." What does "eating well" _____ ? It means eating the right kinds of food.

2. The Food Pyramid is a _____ for eating well. It tells people a good way to eat.

3. A food _____ has more than one kind of food in it. For example, the milk group has yogurt and ice cream in it, too.

4. The six parts of the pyramid are not all the same _____.
   Some are big, and some are small.

5. Is it true that people in the United States eat this way? Or do they
   _____ do something different?

C **Complete the sentences about the pictures. Write *different*, *grow*, or *shows*.**

1. Young children _____ quickly.

2. These nuts are all _____.

3. This map _____ where to go.

D **Complete the sentences with the words in the box.**

different	groups	grow	size

1. Does your hair _____ fast?
2. Flowers don't all smell the same. They have _____ smells.
3. She has small feet. What _____ shoes does she wear?
4. Sometimes the students work with a partner, and sometimes they
   work in _____ of three or four.

E   **Complete the conversations with the words in the box.**

means	plans	really	show

1. **A:** John says he is 21 years old.

    B: I know, but it's not true. He's _____ 19.

2. **A:** I don't know this word *quick*. Do you?

    B: Yes, it _____ "fast."

3. **A:** What do you think of the _____ for the new school?

    B: I don't know enough about them. I need more details.

4. **A:** Is that a book about Japan?

    B: Yes, the photos _____ some beautiful places you can visit.

DEVELOPING YOUR SKILLS

The Topic and the Main Idea

A   Go back to page 45 and read "The Food Pyramid" again.

B   Answer the questions about the topic and the main idea of the reading.

1. What is the topic of the reading? Check (✓) your answer.

    ☐ **a.** Favorite foods in the United States

    ☐ **b.** Good foods for children

    ☐ **c.** A plan for eating well

2. One sentence gives the main idea of the reading. The other three sentences give details from the reading. Write *main idea* or *detail* on the line.

    _____*detail*_____ **a.** The six food groups in the Food Pyramid are different sizes.

    _____ **b.** There is no tea or coffee in the Food Pyramid.

    _____ **c.** The Food Pyramid shows one plan for eating well.

    _____ **d.** Cheese and yogurt are in the milk group.

Scanning the Reading

Scan the reading on page 45. Find the words to complete the sentences.

1. Children have to eat well to _____.
2. The Food Pyramid has _____ parts.
3. These parts are for different food _____.
4. The first part is for _____.
5. The meat and _____ group includes fish and eggs.
6. The part for oil is _____, meaning, "Don't eat a lot of oil."
7. There is no coffee, tea, or _____ in the Food Pyramid.
8. Children learn about the Food Pyramid _____.

Summarizing the Reading

A **Match the beginning and the end of each sentence.**

__c__ **1.** People have to eat well

____ **2.** The Food Pyramid is

____ **3.** It has six parts

____ **4.** It tells how much

____ **5.** Most people in the United States

a. one plan for eating well.

b. to eat of the different kinds of food.

c. to feel good.

d. know about this plan.

e. for six different food groups.

B **Copy the sentences to complete the summary.**

People have to eat well to feel good. The

Discussing the Reading

Talk about these questions with your class.

1. Which is the second biggest food group in the Food Pyramid? Which group is third? Fourth? Fifth?

2. Some kinds of food and drink are not part of the Food Pyramid. What three examples does the reading give? What other examples can you think of?

3. Look at the picture of the Food Pyramid on page 45. It shows a person running up stairs. Why do you think the person is in the picture?

4. Does the Food Pyramid show how people eat in your country? What is the same, and what is different?

1. _____ grains
2. _____
3. _____
4. _____
5. _____
6. ___ oils ___

Using New Words

Work alone or with a partner. Complete the sentences. Then copy your sentences on a piece of paper.

1. I like many **different** kinds of _____.

2. I can **show** you a picture of _____.

3. What does the word "_____" **mean**? It means _____.

4. People sometimes buy _____ when they do not **really** need to.

5. I have **plans** for _____.

Writing

 A Get ready for a dictation. Practice writing these sentences.

1. It is important to eat well.
2. Eat different kinds of food every day.
3. What does this word mean?
4. These shoes are not the right size.

Close your book. Take a piece of paper. Your teacher will say the sentences. Listen and write the sentences.

B On a piece of paper, write the names of three or four food groups. Write sentences about foods in these groups that you like and do not like.

Food group: _____

    I like _____ and _____ .

    I do not like _____ or _____ .

Example:

1. Food group: fruit _____
   _____ I like oranges and blueberries. _____
   _____ I do not like grapefruit or bananas. _____
2. Food group: _____

Wrap-up

REVIEWING VOCABULARY

Circle the correct word to complete the sentence.

1. Many _____ of fruit and vegetables grow in California.
   - **a.** kinds
   - **b.** plans
   - **c.** details

2. I eat the _____ thing for lunch every day: pizza.
   - **a.** most
   - **b.** size
   - **c.** same

3. I _____ a cup of tea, please.
   - **a.** show
   - **b.** would like
   - **c.** grow

4. A: What does the word *watermelon* _____?
   B: A watermelon is a kind of fruit.
   - **a.** meal
   - **b.** may
   - **c.** mean

5. There is a big _____ of apples on the table.
   - **a.** bowl
   - **b.** plan
   - **c.** smell

6. It's important to start the day with a good _____.
   - **a.** different
   - **b.** breakfast
   - **c.** box

7. I would like to buy these shoes, but I don't _____ need them.
   - **a.** snack
   - **b.** group
   - **c.** really

8. _____ it will rain. I don't know.
   - **a.** Also
   - **b.** Maybe
   - **c.** Quick

EXPANDING VOCABULARY

The Suffix -er

Sometimes you can add -er to the end of a word. It changes the word's meaning. Here are three examples:

teach + -er = teacher, a person who teaches
write + -er = writer, a person who writes (Look at the spelling: just one e.)
swim + -er = swimmer, a person who swims (Look at the spelling: mm.)

A **Look at these words. Take away the -er. Complete the sentence with the new word.**

1. hitter   He can _____ hit _____ a baseball very well.

2. rider   Can you _____ ride _____ a bicycle?

3. user   Do you _____ your right hand or your left when you write?

4. shopper   Where do you _____ for clothes?

5. dancer   She loves to _____ .

6. planner   He likes to _____ parties.

B **Add -er to the words in the box. Use the new words to complete the sentences.**

| begin | drive | grow | play | read | sing | work | write |

1. She works for a newspaper. She is a _____ writer _____ .

2. His sport is volleyball. He is a volleyball _____ .

3. She drives well. She is a good _____ .

4. He is just starting to study English. He is a _____ .

5. He does his job well. He is a good _____ .

6. He has 3,000 orange trees in California. He is a _____ .

7. I like to read, but I am not a fast _____.

8. Listen to this music! It's a new group from Brazil with a great
_____.

A PUZZLE

Complete the sentences and the puzzle. Look at the word lists on pages 32, 39, and 46 for help.

Across

3. What _s_____ box do you need for the books?

4. My new school is _d_____ from my old school.

5. Jack is studying Spanish. He is _a_____ studying Chinese.

6. It _m_____ rain, but I don't think it will.

7. I'm hungry. I think I'll have a _s_____.

8. What are you cooking? It _s_____ great!

Down

1. We may have dinner at home, or _____maybe_____ we will go out to eat.

2. _W_____ you like a drink?

3. This map _s_____ all the streets in the city.

4. I don't know every _d_____ of the plan, just the main parts of it.

6. Do you eat three _m_____ a day?

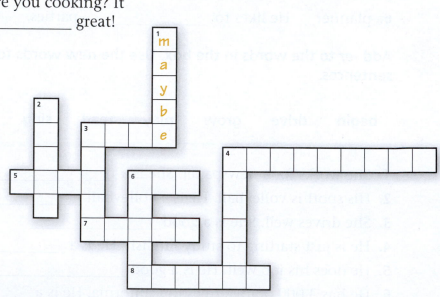

EXTRA READING

Popcorn

1   Do you like popcorn? Most people in the United States do. Every year, they eat more than 200 cups of it per person.[1] That is a lot of popcorn!

2   Most of the time, they eat it for a snack at home. But they get popcorn in other places, too. They buy boxes of it at baseball or basketball games. They also get it at the movies. Many U.S. movie theaters[2] smell like popcorn.

3   Popcorn is easy to make. All you need are some popcorn kernels[3] and some hot oil. The hot oil makes the kernels pop. That is because every kernel has a little water in it. When the water gets hot, steam[4] makes the kernel pop.

4   Popcorn kernels come in different sizes and colors. You can buy white, yellow, red, purple, or black kernels. After it pops, the popcorn is always white.

5   Many people put salt on their popcorn. Some like it with butter, too. Others like popcorn with sugar on it.

6   Would you like a good quick snack? Have a bowl of popcorn!

[1] *per person* = for every person

[2] a *movie theater* = a building where you can see a film

[3] *popcorn kernels*

[4] *steam*

Comprehension Check

Read these sentences about the reading. Circle T (true) or F (false).

1. People in the United States eat a lot of popcorn.   T   F

2. It takes a long time to make popcorn.   T   F

3. The water in popcorn makes it pop when it gets
   hot.   T   F

4. All popcorn is white or yellow.   T   F

5. People in the United States eat popcorn with most
   meals.   T   F

Scanning the Reading

Scan the reading "Popcorn." Find the words to complete the sentences.

1. Every year, people in the United States eat more than
   _____ of popcorn per person.

2. Most people in the United States eat popcorn at _____.

3. Many U.S. _____ smell like popcorn.

4. People cook popcorn in hot _____.

5. You can buy popcorn kernels of different _____ and
   _____.

6. People sometimes put _____, _____, or
   _____ on popcorn.

The Main Idea of the Reading

One sentence gives the main idea of the reading. The other three
sentences give details from the reading. Write *main idea* or *detail* on
the line.

_____*detail*_____ a. Some people put sugar on their popcorn.

_____ b. Many people like to eat popcorn when they watch
                     a movie.

_____ c. Most people eat popcorn out of a box or a bowl.

_____ d. Many people in the United States like popcorn as a
                     snack.

Vocabulary Self-Test 1

Choose an answer to complete each sentence. Circle the letter of your answer.

Example:

Breakfast is my favorite _____ of the day.

a. box   **b.** meal   **c.** lunch

1. To learn to speak a new language, you have to _____.

    a. grow   **b.** smell   **c.** practice

2. These shoes are _____ eight.

    a. bowl   **b.** size   **c.** plan

3. I'd like a pizza with _____ cheese, please. I love cheese!

    a. early   **b.** tired   **c.** extra

4. There are buses in _____ cities.

    a. most   **b.** everything   **c.** really

5. The children eat a _____ after school.

    a. beginner   **b.** snack   **c.** group

6. What does the word *early* _____?

    a. mean   **b.** would like   **c.** has to

7. Please put your paper here, with the _____ papers.

    a. other   **b.** afraid   **c.** also

8. I like chocolate ice cream, and she does, _____.

    a. because   **b.** too   **c.** favorite

9. Can you _____ me how to do it?

    a. spend   **b.** show   **c.** quick

10. I know a little Russian, but I can't speak it _____.
    a. for example   b. maybe   c. well

11. She has a lot to do on weekends. She's always _____.
    a. different   b. busy   c. every

12. You don't have to pay much for the bus. It's _____ a dollar.
    a. enough   b. the same   c. just

13. He isn't here now, but he _____ come later.
    a. may   b. use   c. learn

14. I have _____ good friends, not many.
    a. more   b. a few   c. ready

15. Tell me more! I want all the _____.
    a. kinds   b. details   c. breakfasts

See the Answer Key on page 150.

HAVING FUN

An Easy Game

Two businessmen playing Rock, Paper, Scissors

GETTING READY TO READ

Talk about these questions with your class.

1. Look at the photo. What do you see?

2. What do you think: Which of these games are for children? Which games are for older people? Which games are for everyone?

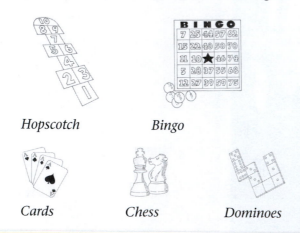

Hopscotch   Bingo

Cards   Chess   Dominoes

READ TO FIND OUT: How do you play the game Rock, Paper, Scissors?

READING

Look at the pictures and the words next to the reading. Then read. Do not stop to use a dictionary.

An Easy Game

1   Do you know the game Rock, Paper, Scissors? Maybe you know it by a different name. People call it Ching Chong Cha in South Africa. They call it Ca-Chi-Pun in Chile. In Korea, it is called Kawi Bawi Bo. People young and old play this game in countries all **around** the **world**. It is an easy game to play because it has just a few **rules**.

2   There are two players in the game. They play the game standing up. **Each** player **holds** one hand closed. First, the players move their arms up and down, saying "One, two, three." When they say "three," each player makes a hand gesture.[1]

[1] a *gesture* = a hand or head movement that means something

3   There are three gestures a player can make: rock, paper, or scissors. The three gestures look like this:

Rock   *Paper*   *Scissors*

4   When the two players make two different gestures, who wins? Rock **beats** scissors. Scissors beats paper. Paper beats rock. Sometimes **both** players make the same gesture. Then nobody wins.

5   Each time the players make their gestures, it is a "throw." There have to be three or more throws in a game. The player who wins two out of three throws is the winner. **Try** it with a friend.

6   Rock, Paper, Scissors is easy to learn and fun to play. To learn more about it, try going online.[2]

[2] *online* = on the Internet

Quick Comprehension Check

A   **Read these sentences about the reading. Circle T (true) or F (false).**

1. Rock, Paper, Scissors is a game just for children.   T   F

2. People play this game in many places.   T   F

3. A person needs to use two hands to play.   T   F

4. One player goes first and then the other player.   T   F

5. You can learn more about this game on the
    Internet.   T   F

B   **Can you answer the Read to Find Out question on page 60?**

EXPLORING VOCABULARY

A   **Find the words in bold in "An Easy Game" on page 61. Write them in the list. Use alphabetical order.**

1. around _____   5. _____

2. _____   6. _____

3. _____   7. _____

4. _____   8. _____

B   **Complete the sentences with the words in the box. The sentences are about the reading.**

around	beats	both	rules	try

1. People play Rock, Paper, Scissors in many different countries. You can
    find the game all _____ the world.

2. Every game has _____. They say what players can and
    cannot do.

3. The rules of the game say, "Rock _____ scissors." When I
    throw rock and you throw scissors, I win.

4. Sometimes the two players make the same gesture. For example, _____ players throw paper.

5. When you _____ a new game, you play it for the first time. Maybe you'll like it and maybe you won't.

C **Complete the sentences about the picture. Write *each*, *holding*, or *world*.**

These three athletes come

from different parts of the

_____. _____
(1)   (2)

athlete is _____ a ball.
(3)

D **Complete the sentences with the words in the box.**

both	each	rules	world

1. We have 20 students and 20 pencils. There is one pencil for _____ student.

2. This is a big bowl. You need to hold it in _____ hands.

3. It is not easy to learn the spelling _____ for English words.

4. Is Beijing the biggest city in the _____?

E   **Complete the conversations with the words in the box.**

around	beating	hold	try

1. **A:** Are the Red Sox winning the game?

   B: Yes, they're _____ the Yankees, 5 to 4.

2. **A:** Can I help you with those bags?

   B: Would you just _____ the door open for me? Thanks!

3. **A:** Can you help me with my French homework?

   B: I'll _____ to help you, but I don't know much French.

4. **A:** What does the word *island* mean?

   B: An island is a place with water all _____ it.

An island

DEVELOPING YOUR SKILLS

The Topic and the Main Idea

A   **Go back to page 61 and read "An Easy Game" again.**

B   **Answer the questions about the topic and the main idea of the reading.**

1. What is the topic of the reading? Check (✓) your answer.

   ☐ **a.** Games on the Internet

   ☐ **b.** Rock, Paper, Scissors

   ☐ **c.** Games around the world

2. What is the main idea of the reading? Check (✓) your answer.

   ☐ **a.** Rock, Paper, Scissors is a game with just a few easy rules.

   ☐ **b.** Young and old people can play the same games.

   ☐ **c.** People know Rock, Paper, Scissors in many places.

Scanning the Reading

A **Scan the reading on page 61. Find the words to complete the sentences.**

1. Rock, Paper, Scissors is called Ching Chong Cha in
   _____.

2. The same game is called Ca-Chi-Pun in _____.

3. The same game is called Kawi Bawi Bo in _____.

4. Both _____ people and _____ people play
   this game.

5. The _____ of the game are easy to learn.

6. Each player uses his or her hand to make a _____ .

7. It is important for players to make their gestures at the same
   _____.

8. You can find out more about the game on the _____.

B **Complete the diagram. Write the names of the three gestures in the three places.**

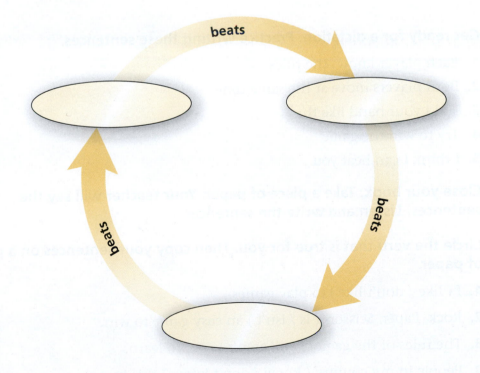

Discussing the Reading

Talk about these questions with your class.

1. The reading says that many people play Rock, Paper, Scissors. Who are they?

2. Do people in your country know this game? Do you play it?

3. What are the rules of the game? Tell how many players there are, what they have to do, and how someone wins.

Using New Words

Work alone or with a partner. Complete the sentences. Then copy your sentences on a piece of paper.

1. I know the **rules** for _____.

2. **Both** my mother and my father _____.

3. I want to **try** to _____.

4. I think _____ can **beat** _____.

5. _____ **around** the **world**.

Writing

 Get ready for a dictation. Practice writing these sentences.

1. Each player knows the rules.

2. Both players move at the same time.

3. Hold your hand like this.

4. Try to win the game.

5. I think I can beat you.

Close your book. Take a piece of paper. Your teacher will say the sentences. Listen and write the sentences.

B **Circle the verb that is true for you. Then copy your sentences on a piece of paper.**

1. I (like / don't like) to play games.

2. Rock, Paper, Scissors (is / isn't) an easy game to win.

3. The rules of the game (are / aren't) easy to learn.

4. People in my country (know / don't know) this game.

5. I (play / don't play) other kinds of games.

Example:

1. I don't like to play games.

A New and Different Sport

Get that disc!

GETTING READY TO READ

Talk about these questions with your class.

1. Look at the photo. What do you see?

2. Match the names and pictures of these sports: *baseball, basketball, football, skating, soccer, tennis.*

a.   b.   c.   d.   e.   f.

3. Do you like any of these sports?

> **READ TO FIND OUT:** How is Ultimate Frisbee different from other sports?

READING

Look at the words and pictures next to the reading. Then read. Do not stop to use a dictionary.

A New and Different Sport

1   Does everyone in the world know soccer? It **seems** that way! Most people know basketball, too. Not as many people know Ultimate Frisbee because it is a new sport. People just started playing it in the 1960s. It is like other **team** sports in many ways. In one important way, it is very different.

2   Ultimate, like soccer, is played on a big **field**. There are two teams, and each team has seven players. One team tries to get the disc[1] to the other end of the field. The other team tries to stop them. The player holding the disc cannot run or walk with it. He or she has to stop and throw it. The player's teammates[2] try to **catch** the disc. Ultimate players, like soccer and basketball players, do a lot of running.

3   All sports have rules, but sometimes a player does not play by the rules. In soccer or basketball, a referee[3] stops the game. Then the referee tells the players what to do. Ultimate is different. There are no referees. The players stop the game and talk about the **problem**. They have to **agree** on what to do. Then they start the game again.

4   Today, men, women, and children in more than 40 countries **enjoy** playing Ultimate Frisbee. The sport is growing fast. Maybe there is a game of Ultimate **happening** near you.

[1] an Ultimate *disc*

[2] a *teammate* = a player on the same team

[3] a *referee*

Quick Comprehension Check

(A) **Read these sentences about the reading. Circle T (true) or F (false).**

1. Many people do not know about Ultimate Frisbee.   T   F

2. Ultimate is a game for two players with a Frisbee.   T   F

3. One player takes the disc and runs with it.   T   F

4. People play Ultimate only in the United States.   T   F

5. People play Ultimate with no referees.   T   F

(B) **Can you answer the Read to Find Out question on page 67?**

EXPLORING VOCABULARY

(A) **Find the words in bold in "A New and Different Sport" on page 68. Write them in the list. Use alphabetical order.**

1. agree

2. _____

3. _____

4. _____

5. _____

6. _____

7. _____

8. _____

(B) **Complete the sentences with the words in the box. The sentences are about the reading.**

agree	enjoy	happening	problem	seems

1. It isn't really true that everyone in the world knows soccer. It just _____ true.

2. Sometimes a player doesn't play by the rules. That is a _____. It makes the other team unhappy.

3. When there is a problem, Ultimate players stop the game and talk. They have to _____ on what to do about the problem. They need to have the same idea about what to do.

4. People in more than 40 countries like playing Ultimate. Many men like this sport, and many women _____ it, too.

5. People play Ultimate in many places. Maybe a game is _____ right now near you.

C **Complete the sentences about the picture. Write *catch*, *field*, or *teams*.**

The picture shows two boys from different baseball _____.
(1)
They are on the _____. One
(2)
boy is trying to _____ the
(3)
ball.

D **Complete the sentences with the words in the box.**

catch	enjoy	field	team

1. People play Ultimate Frisbee on a long _____.
2. A soccer _____ has 11 players on the field.
3. I like to go see new places, but I don't _____ flying.
4. Use both hands to _____ the ball.

E **Complete the conversations with the words in the box.**

agree	happening	problem	seem

1. **A:** I think we need a computer. What do you think?
   B: I _____.
2. **A:** Ed and Marta _____ happy.
   B: Yes, they do, but they really aren't.

3. A: Why is Robert taking the bus?

 B: He's having a _____ with his car.

4. A: Can I call you back later? I'm watching the game.

 B: What's _____? Who's winning?

DEVELOPING YOUR SKILLS

The Topic and the Main Idea

A Go back to page 68 and read "A New and Different Sport" again.

B Answer the questions about the topic and the main idea of the reading.

1. What is the topic of the reading? Check (✓) your answer.

 ☐ **a.** The sport of Ultimate Frisbee

 ☐ **b.** Sports around the world

 ☐ **c.** Team sports

2. What is the main idea of the reading? Check (✓) your answer.

 ☐ **a.** More people know soccer than Ultimate Frisbee.

 ☐ **b.** In the game of Ultimate Frisbee, there is a lot of throwing and catching the disc.

 ☐ **c.** Ultimate Frisbee is like soccer and basketball in some ways but very different, too.

Giving Details

Answer these questions about the reading on a piece of paper.

1. When did people start playing the sport of Ultimate Frisbee?
 in the 1960s

2. What two other examples of team sports does the reading give?

3. How many people play on an Ultimate team?

4. What does the player with the disc try to do?

5. Who starts and stops the game in soccer or basketball?

6. Who starts and stops the game in Ultimate Frisbee?

7. Is Ultimate a game for men, for women, or for both men and women?

8. How many countries have people that play Ultimate Frisbee?

Summarizing the Reading

Complete the summary of the reading on page 68. Use *catch*, *disc*, *field*, *referees*, and *team*.

Ultimate Frisbee is a fast-growing sport. It is a _____ sport,
(1)
like soccer and basketball. Ultimate is played on a _____,
(2)
like soccer. One team tries to get the _____ to the other end
(3)
of the field. The other team tries to stop them. Players have to throw and

_____ the disc. There is a lot of running in Ultimate, as in
(4)
basketball and soccer. Ultimate is different from those two sports in one

important way. There are no _____.
(5)

Discussing the Reading

Talk about these questions with your class.

1. How are Ultimate Frisbee and soccer the same? Write your answers in
the diagram under *Both*. How are the two sports different? Write your
answers under each sport.

ULTIMATE FRISBEE   BOTH   SOCCER

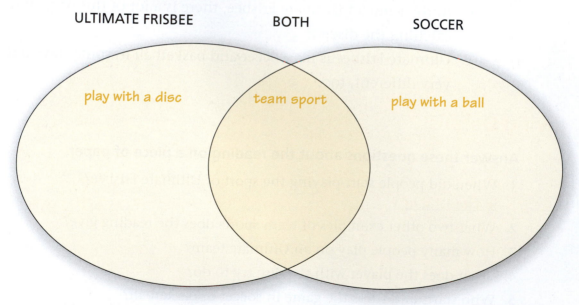

play with a disc   team sport   play with a ball

2. List some other sports for two teams, and list some sports for two people
(for example, boxing and tennis). Think about people playing these
sports with no referees. Do you think this is a good idea? Tell why or
why not.

Using New Words

Work alone or with a partner. Complete the sentences. Then copy your sentences on a piece of paper.

1. I **enjoy** watching _____.
2. People play _____ on a **field**.
3. Sometimes I have **problems** with _____.
4. _____ and I sometimes don't **agree** about _____.
5. What **happens** when _____?

Writing

A **Get ready for a dictation. Practice writing these sentences.**

1. People play sports around the world.
2. Many people enjoy watching sports.
3. Do you watch sports on TV?
4. Do you have a favorite sport?

Close your book. Take a piece of paper. Your teacher will say the sentences. Listen and write the sentences.

B **Write your answers to these questions on a piece of paper.**

1. What sports do people like in your country?
2. Do you like to play sports?
3. Do you watch sports on TV?
4. Do you have a favorite sport?

Examples:

1. People in my country like soccer and auto racing.
2. I do not like to play sports.
3. I sometimes watch the Olympics on TV.
4. I do not have a favorite sport.

CHAPTER

9

Collectors

Trading card collectors and a doll collector

GETTING READY TO READ

Talk about these questions with your class.

1. Look at the photos. What do you see?

2. Do you know people who collect any of these things?

butterflies

teddy bears

earrings

3. What other kinds of things do people collect?

READ TO FIND OUT: Who likes to collect things?

74

READING

Look at the words and pictures next to the reading. Then read. Do not stop to use a dictionary.

Collectors

1   Many people like to **collect** things. They collect all kinds of things, from comic books[1] to teacups to cars. Why do they do it? Most collectors will tell you, "Because it's fun." Some say, "I **hope** to make some money."

2   Other people may **laugh** and say, "Collecting? No, that's not for me! I'm not a collector." Is that really true? Many of us collect things **without** thinking about it.

3   Small children do not think about it, but they are natural[2] collectors. They **pick up** little things they see. For example, a little boy finds a nice stone or a shell.[3] Then he finds some more. He takes them home, and he has the start of a collection.

4   Older children collect things, too—teddy bears, for example. Some collect trading cards with pictures of their favorite athletes.[4] Many enjoy collecting the same things as their friends. When they get something new, they tell their friends about it and show them. These children enjoy playing with their things **together**.

5   Men and women may collect things that make them **remember** being children. Jared Millen of Milwaukee, Wisconsin, collects lunch boxes. When he was a child, he always **carried** a lunch box to school. Now he has more than 300 of them. Some people will pay a lot for an old lunch box. In 2005, a 1954 Superman lunch box sold on eBay[5] for more than $4,000.

6   Are you a collector? Maybe your answer at first is no, but think again. Maybe you have a lot of photos, music, T-shirts, or earrings. Then you are a collector, too.

[1] a *comic book*

[2] *natural* = needing no teaching

[3] *stones* and a *shell*

[4] *athletes* = people who play sports

[5] *eBay* = a place to buy and sell online

Quick Comprehension Check

A   **Read these sentences about the reading. Circle T (true) or F (false).**

1. A collector has many things of the same kind.   T   F

2. Men, women, and children can be collectors.   T   F

3. Small children do not have collections.   T   F

4. Older children often show their collections to
   their friends.   T   F

5. Most collectors try to get a lot of money for
   their things.   T   F

B   **Can you answer the Read to Find Out question on page 74?**

EXPLORING VOCABULARY

A   **Find the words in bold in "Collectors" on page 75. Write them in the list. Use alphabetical order.**

1. carried   5. _____

2. _____   6. _____

3. _____   7. _____

4. _____   8. _____

B   **Complete the sentences with the words in the box. The sentences are about the reading.**

collect	hope	remember	together	without

1. Many people like to _____ things. This means to get a lot
   of things of one kind and put them all in one place. A person who
   collects things is called "a collector." The group of things is called "a
   collection."

2. Some people collect things because they _____ to make
   money. They want this to happen.

3. Many of us collect things _____ thinking about making a collection. We do it, but we do not think about it.

4. Most children like to play with others. They like to play _____.

5. Some people collect things that make them _____ being children. These people think back to the time when they were young.

C   **Complete the sentences about the pictures. Write *carrying*, *laughing*, or *picking up*.**

1. She is _____ a shell from the beach.

2. He is _____ a lunch box to work.

3. They are _____.

D   **Complete the conversations with the words in the box.**

carry	laughing	remember	without

1. A: Do you know that girl?

   B: Yes, but I can't _____ her name.

2. A: Would you like some help?

   B: Thanks! I need to _____ these boxes up to the fourth floor.

3. A: Ha ha ha ha ha!

   B: What's so funny? Why are you _____?

4. A: Is it cold today?

   B: Yes, it is. Don't go out _____ a coat and hat.

E   Complete the sentences with the words in the box.

collect	hope	pick up	together

1. The players on a team need to work _____.
2. Soccer players use their feet. They cannot _____ the ball with their hands.
3. They _____ stamps from around the world.
4. I _____ my team will win.

DEVELOPING YOUR SKILLS

The Topic and the Main Idea

A   Go back to page 75 and read "Collectors" again.

B   Answer the questions about the topic and the main idea of the reading.

1. What is the topic of the reading? Check (✓) your answer.
   - ☐ **a.** Collecting for children
   - ☐ **b.** People who collect things
   - ☐ **c.** Making money from a collection

2. What is the main idea of the reading? Check (✓) your answer.
   - ☐ **a.** Collecting is fun for many men, women, and children.
   - ☐ **b.** Collectors are people with a lot of money and free time.
   - ☐ **c.** There are a few easy rules for starting a collection.

Finding Examples

Complete the chart. Give examples from the reading and think of more examples of your own.

		Collectors		
		Small Children	Older Children	Men and Women
Examples of Things People Collect	From the Reading	little stones shells		
	Your Ideas			

Giving Details

Answer these questions about the reading on a piece of paper.

1. Why do most people collect things? ___because it's fun___
2. What do some people hope to get from collecting things?
3. Why do some men and women collect lunch boxes?
4. How many lunch boxes does Jared Millen have?
5. How much money did someone pay for a 1954 Superman lunch box?
6. Where did the person buy the lunch box?
7. In what year did this happen?

Discussing the Reading

Talk about these questions with your class.

1. What kinds of things do children collect? Did you collect things when you were a child?
2. Why do men and women collect things? Give answers from the reading, and also tell about people you know.
3. Do you collect things now? What would you like to collect?

Using New Words

Work alone or with a partner. Complete the sentences. Then copy your answers on a piece of paper.

1. I **carry** _____ in my (backpack / wallet / handbag).
2. I would like to **collect** _____.
3. It is sometimes hard for me to **remember** _____.
4. I **hope** to _____ tomorrow.
5. I **laugh** when _____.

Writing

 Get ready for a dictation. Practice writing these sentences.

1. People collect all kinds of things.
2. Small children pick up little things.
3. Many men and women are collectors.
4. Some of them spend a lot of money.

Close your book. Take a piece of paper. Your teacher will say the sentences. Listen and write the sentences.

B **Give one or more answers to each question. Write your sentences on a piece of paper.**

1. What, or who, makes you laugh?
2. What do you and your friends like to do together?
3. What will you always remember?

Examples:

1. My little brother makes me laugh.
2. My friends and I like to go dancing. We like to study together.
3. I will always remember my friends from high school.

Wrap-up

REVIEWING VOCABULARY

Circle the correct word to complete the sentence.

1. There are 12 students and 12 computers. That means one computer for _____ student.
   a. both   **b.** each   **c.** catch

2. The players on a team all have to work _____.
   a. rule   **b.** field   **c.** together

3. She _____ happy today.
   a. seems   **b.** beats   **c.** problems

4. You need to learn the _____ to play the game.
   a. rules   **b.** worlds   **c.** laughs

5. I like it when good things _____ to nice people.
   a. remember   **b.** carry   **c.** happen

6. I _____ that we'll have nice weather this weekend.
   a. enjoy   **b.** hope   **c.** collect

7. They _____ their little boy and carry him when he is tired of walking.
   a. try   **b.** pick up   **c.** team

8. Will you please _____ the baby for me?
   a. without   **b.** agree   **c.** hold

EXPANDING VOCABULARY

Nouns

There are many different kinds of words. A **noun** is one kind of word.
It is a word for a person, a place, a thing, or an idea. Most nouns can
be singular (*book*) or plural (*books*).

What Is a Noun?		Examples of Nouns
Nouns are words for	people:	boy, police, drivers, George
	places:	airport, classroom, fields, Tokyo
	things:	bicycle, pen, bowls, Honda
	ideas:	time, light, rules, size

Each sentence has one noun. Find and circle the noun.

1. She is a good student.
2. Do you eat a big breakfast?
3. They are beginners.
4. You are a fast learner.
5. My team is winning.
6. What is in the box?
7. I think it is a good plan.
8. Our group is small.
9. Would you like a snack?
10. They are flying around the world.

A PUZZLE

Complete the sentences and the puzzle. Look at the word lists on pages 62, 69, and 76 for help.

Across

1. I like my coffee black. That means w_____ milk or cream.
2. I like that actor, but I can't r_____ his name.
3. Before they practice, the players run a_____ the field.
5. I will t_____ to get there early.
6. I e_____ watching sports on TV.
7. I h_____ you have a good time at the party.
8. His stories always make me l_____.

Down

1. They are flying around the _____world_____.
3. She thinks they can spend the money, but her husband does not a_____.
4. Henry has two sisters, and they are b_____ in college.
5. Fatima and Carmen ride the bus t_____.

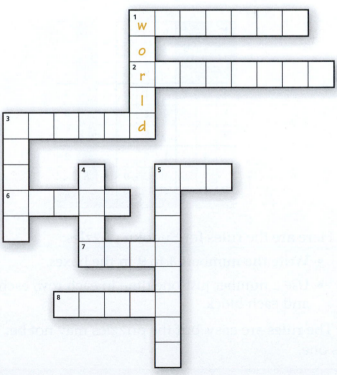

EXTRA READING

Do You Like Puzzles?

1   Puzzles can be a lot of fun. There are many different kinds. Some use pictures. Some use words or numbers. Three popular[1] kinds are jigsaw, crossword, and Sudoku puzzles.

2   A jigsaw puzzle has many small pieces. A piece looks something like this:

Each piece has a part of a picture on it. Put all the pieces together and you will see the picture.

3   On page 83, there is a crossword puzzle. It is a game of words. This kind of puzzle is very popular in the United States. You can find crosswords in newspapers and on the Internet. Millions[2] of people try to do the crosswords in *The New York Times* newspaper.

4   You can find Sudoku puzzles in newspapers and online, too. Sudoku puzzles use numbers. Here is an example of a Sudoku puzzle.

[1] *popular* = liked by many people

[2] a *million* = 1,000,000

1		3	6		4			
	9	8	2					
2				9	5		3	
		2		1				3
3			9	2				4
9				8				
	4		1	5				2
					9	8	6	
			7		2	1		9

5   Here are the rules for Sudoku puzzles:
  • Write the numbers 1 to 9 in the boxes.
  • Use a number just one time in each row, each column, and each block.

The rules are easy, but the puzzles may not be. Try to do this one.

Comprehension Check

Read these sentences about the reading. Circle T (true) or F (false).

1. There are many different kinds of puzzles.   T   F

2. There are crossword puzzles in this book.   T   F

3. You can find jigsaw puzzles in U.S. newspapers.   T   F

4. A Sudoku puzzle is a game of words.   T   F

5. You need to learn many rules to do a Sudoku
   puzzle.   T   F

Scanning the Reading

Find the words to complete the sentences about the reading.

1. A puzzle may use pictures, _____, or _____.
2. A jigsaw puzzle has many small _____.
3. A crossword puzzle is a game of _____.
4. You can find crossword puzzles in _____ and on the
   _____.
5. Sudoku puzzles use _____.
6. Write the numbers _____ to _____ in the boxes of a Sudoku
   puzzle.

Topics of Paragraphs

Match the paragraphs and their topics. Write each paragraph topic in the right place.

Do You Like Puzzles?	
Paragraph 1	kinds of puzzles
Paragraph 2	
Paragraph 3	
Paragraph 4	
Paragraph 5	

Topics of Paragraphs
rules for Sudoku puzzles
Sudoku puzzles
jigsaw puzzles
crossword puzzles
✓kinds of puzzles

The Main Idea of the Reading

What is the main idea of the reading? Check (✓) your answer.

☐ **a.** You can find crosswords and Sudoku puzzles in newspapers and online.

☐ **b.** Three popular kinds of puzzles are jigsaw, crossword, and Sudoku puzzles.

☐ **c.** Puzzles are fun for people young and old.

UNIT 4

SHOPPING

10

Mystery Shoppers

A customer and a salesperson

GETTING READY TO READ

Talk about these questions with your class.

1. Look at the photo. What do you see?

2. What do you think about statements a–d? Circle a number from 1 to 4. Then find out what your classmates think.

	Yes, I agree.	← Sometimes →		No, I don't agree.
a. It is fun to spend time in stores.	1	2	3	4
b. I am a good shopper.	1	2	3	4
c. I like to shop for other people.	1	2	3	4
d. Salespeople in stores are a big help.	1	2	3	4

READ TO FIND OUT: What is a mystery shopper?

READING

Look at the words and picture next to the reading. Then read. Do not stop to use a dictionary.

Mystery Shoppers

1   Nina likes to shop. She goes shopping **almost** every day. Maybe you think she spends a lot of money, but she does not. People pay her to shop! Yes, Nina makes money when she goes shopping. She is not just a customer[1]. Nina works as a mystery shopper.

2   A mystery shopper's job is to go into a store and learn about it. Is it a nice place to shop? Is it easy to find things? Are the **salespeople** doing a good job? A mystery shopper buys something in the store. He or she may secretly[2] take pictures, too. Then the mystery shopper writes a **report**. The report goes to the people who **own** the store.

3   In the United States, store owners **often** use mystery shoppers. They pay them more than one billion[3] dollars a year. They use them to learn about their stores. Restaurant owners use them, too. Mystery shoppers can help store and restaurant owners **understand** their customers.

4   Mark is a mystery shopper, too. He likes going to new stores and spending the store owner's money. He also likes shopping for new products,[4] most of all for electronics.[5] Mark says, "Sometimes I can **keep** the things I buy." He can take his wife to nice restaurants, too. "And we pay **nothing**!" he says.

5   Nina and Mark, like most mystery shoppers, do this work part-time.[6] These jobs do not pay a lot, **so** most mystery shoppers have to work at other jobs, too. Mark says, "You can't **get rich** as a mystery shopper, but it can be fun."

[1] a *customer* = someone who buys something from a store or a company

[2] *secretly* = without people knowing

[3] *one billion* = 1,000,000,000

[4] *products* = things made to sell

[5] *electronics*

[6] *part-time* = not many hours each week

Quick Comprehension Check

A   **Read these sentences about the reading. Circle T (true) or F (false).**

1. Mystery shopping is a job.   T   F

2. A mystery shopper goes shopping and then writes
   about the store.   T   F

3. Most mystery shoppers shop online.   T   F

4. Mystery shoppers sometimes go into restaurants.   T   F

5. Most mystery shoppers need other jobs, too.   T   F

B   **Can you answer the Read to Find Out question on page 88?**

EXPLORING VOCABULARY

A   **Find the words in bold in "Mystery Shoppers" on page 89. Write them in the list. Use alphabetical order.**

1. almost _____   6. _____

2. get rich _____   7. _____

3. _____   8. _____

4. _____   9. _____

5. _____   10. _____

B   **Complete the sentences with the words in the box. The sentences are about the reading.**

| get rich | keep | nothing | often | report | so | understand |

1. A mystery shopper writes about a store or restaurant for the owner.
   The mystery shopper writes a _____.

2. Store and restaurant owners _____ use mystery shoppers.
   They don't always do this, but they do it a lot.

3. Store and restaurant owners use mystery shoppers to learn about their customers. They want to _____ what their customers like and don't like.

4. Mark uses a store owner's money to buy things in the store. Sometimes Mark has to give the things back to the store, but sometimes he can _____ them.

5. Mark does not have to pay for his meals. He pays _____.

6. Nina and Mark don't make much money as mystery shoppers, _____ they need other jobs.

7. Working as a mystery shopper will not help a person make a lot of money. A person who wants to _____ needs a different job.

C Complete the sentences about the pictures. Write *almost*, *owner*, or *salesperson*.

1. This woman has a new car. She is a new car _____. The man is a _____.

2. It is _____ five o'clock.

D Complete the conversations with the words in the box.

almost	getting rich	nothing	salesperson	so

1. **A:** Are the owners of that restaurant making much money?
   B: Yes, they are! They're _____.

2. **A:** I hope you can come to the movies with us this weekend.
   B: I'd like to come, but I have to work, _____ I can't.

3. **A:** How old is Jack?
   B: He's _____ 20. His birthday is next week

4. A: Maria! Here are some nice shoes. Are these what you're looking for?

B: Maybe. Do they come in other colors? I'll ask a _____.

5. A: There's _____ to eat in the house.

B: OK, then, we can go out to eat.

E **Match the beginning and the end of each sentence.**

1. I like going out with my friends.
I _____.

2. Please tell me again. I don't _____.

3. I'm turning on the TV to watch the weather _____.

4. After you buy something, you _____.

5. When I take out a library book, I can _____.

report
understand
own it
often do it
keep it for two weeks

DEVELOPING YOUR SKILLS

The Topic and the Main Idea

A **Go back to page 89 and read "Mystery Shoppers" again.**

B **Answer the questions about the topic and the main idea of the reading.**

1. What is the topic of the reading? Check (✓) your answer.

☐ **a.** Nina and Mark

☐ **b.** Mystery shoppers

☐ **c.** Shopping in stores

2. What is the main idea of the reading? Check (✓) your answer.

☐ **a.** Nina and Mark work as mystery shoppers.

☐ **b.** Mystery shopping is a really great job to have.

☐ **c.** The job of a mystery shopper is to go shopping and write about it.

Reading for Details

A Complete the answers to the questions.

1. What does Nina do? She is a __mystery shopper__.
2. How does Nina feel about shopping? She _____.
3. Who pays Nina to go shopping? _____ pay her.
4. Why do store owners use mystery shoppers? They use them to learn about _____.
5. How much do U.S. store owners spend on mystery shoppers? They spend more than _____ a year.
6. How does Mark feel about being a mystery shopper? He

   _____.

B Read the questions. Circle the answer. Circle "It doesn't say" when the reading does not give the answer.

1. Does Nina go shopping in the evening?   Yes   No   (It doesn't say.)

2. Do mystery shoppers buy things in stores?   Yes   No   It doesn't say.

3. Do mystery shoppers sometimes take pictures?   Yes   No   It doesn't say.

4. Do store and restaurant owners get reports from mystery shoppers?   Yes.   No   It doesn't say.

5. Are most mystery shoppers women?   Yes   No   It doesn't say.

6. Does Mark go shopping every day?   Yes   No   It doesn't say.

7. Does Mark eat in nice restaurants sometimes?   Yes   No   It doesn't say.

8. Can you make a lot of money working as a mystery shopper?   Yes   No   It doesn't say.

Summarizing the Reading

Complete the summary of the reading on page 89. Use *customers*, *learn*, *often*, *owner*, *report*, and *shops*.

A mystery shopper _____ at a store or eats in a restaurant.
                              (1)

Then he or she writes a _____ for the _____.
                               (2)   (3)

Store and restaurant owners _____ use mystery shoppers to
                                       (4)

_____ about their workers and their _____.
        (5)   (6)

Discussing the Reading

Talk about these questions with your class.

1. Why do store and restaurant owners use mystery shoppers? What do they want to learn?

2. How are mystery shoppers and other shoppers the same? Write your answers in the diagram under *Both*. How are they different? Write your answers on each side.

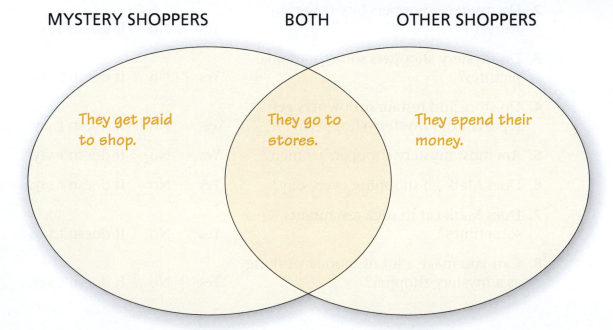

MYSTERY SHOPPERS   BOTH   OTHER SHOPPERS

They get paid to shop.

They go to stores.

They spend their money.

3. What do you think: How do salespeople feel about mystery shoppers? Why?

4. What are the good things about being a mystery shopper? What are the bad parts of the job? Would you like to be a mystery shopper? Tell why or why not.

Using New Words

Work alone or with a partner. Complete the sentences. Then copy your sentences on a piece of paper.

1. I **keep** my money in _____.
2. Many _____ **get rich**.
3. I would like to **own** _____.
4. **Almost** everybody likes _____.
5. I want to _____, **so** I need to

   _____.

Writing

Give one or more answers to each question. On a piece of paper, write your sentences in the form of a paragraph.

1. Do you like shopping?
2. What kinds of things do you shop for?
3. Where do you go shopping?
4. When do you shop?

Example:

   I like shopping. I shop for food, clothes, and things for my son. I often go to the Shop & Save supermarket. Sometimes I go to the Westside Mall. I shop in the evening or on weekends. On weekends, I sometimes go with my sister.

Online Shoppers

CHAPTER 11

Click here when you are ready to buy.

GETTING READY TO READ

Talk about these questions with your class.

1. Look at the photos. What do you see?
2. How many people in the class use computers?
3. How many people in the class use the Internet?
4. How many people in the class use the Internet for shopping?
5. What kinds of things can people buy on the Internet? Make a list.

READ TO FIND OUT: What is an online shopper?

96

READING

Look at the words and picture next to the reading. Then read. Do not stop to use a dictionary.

Online Shoppers

1   Online shoppers are people who use the Internet to shop. With their computers, they can visit stores around the world. They know they can buy **anything** online, from books and music to cars and houses.

2   Online shoppers are not all the same. They use the Internet in different ways. Here are four kinds of online shoppers:

3   1. Newcomers—Newcomers are new to online shopping. It is **hard** for them to understand websites at first.[1] They may be afraid to try new things. They are **usually** happier buying products[2] they know well. For example, a newcomer may shop online for the same kind of shoe he always **wears**.

4   2. Bargain Hunters[3]—What is a bargain? It is something you buy at a great **price**. Bargain hunters go online to look at prices. They love finding good prices for things that are usually **expensive**. They also look online for **information** about prices at local[4] stores.

5   3. Nonstop Shoppers—Nonstop shoppers love to spend time online. They love looking at products and reading about them. They often tell their friends about good websites. They think online shopping is fun.

6   4. Single-minded[5] Shoppers—Single-minded shoppers usually go online to look for just one thing. They find it, **decide** to buy it, and finish quickly. They do not want to spend a lot of time shopping online. For them, it is not fun.

7   Not everyone uses the Internet to shop. Some people just do not like computers. Others **worry** about online shopping. They think it is not **safe** to use their credit cards on the Internet.

8   Do you shop online? Which kind of shopper are you?

[1] *at first* = in the beginning

[2] a *product* = something made to sell

[3] a butterfly *hunter*

[4] *local* = near the place you live

[5] *single-minded* = thinking about just one thing

Quick Comprehension Check

A Read these sentences about the reading. Circle T (true) or F (false).

1. An online shopper uses a computer to buy things.   T   F

2. All online shoppers use the Internet in the same way.   T   F

3. Some people spend a lot of time shopping online.   T   F

4. People can go online just to learn about things.   T   F

5. All online shoppers love to shop.   T   F

B Can you answer the Read to Find Out question on page 96?

EXPLORING VOCABULARY

A Find the words in **bold** in "Online Shoppers" on page 97. Write them in the list. Use alphabetical order.

1. anything _____

2. _____

3. _____

4. _____

5. _____

6. _____

7. _____

8. _____

9. _____

10. _____

B Complete the sentences with the words in the box. The sentences are about the reading.

anything   decide   expensive   hard   information   safe   usually

1. You can use the Internet to buy all kinds of things: clothes, computers, food, TVs, telephones—you can buy _____ online!

2. For newcomers, it can be _____ to understand websites. It is not easy for them, so they need extra time to read them.

3. Most of the time, newcomers don't buy new products online. They don't _____ do this.

4. When you pay just a little for something that is usually _____, you get a bargain.

5. Many people go online to learn about products. They have questions, and they go online to get _____.

6. "Do I want to buy this or not?" Some shoppers take a lot of time to _____. Single-minded shoppers don't.

7. Some people don't want to give their credit card numbers online. They think it may not be _____. They think something bad may happen.

C   **Complete the sentences about the pictures. Write** *price*, *wear*, **or** *worry*.

1. People _____ when their children are sick.

2. They both _____ glasses.

3. The salesperson is looking for the _____ on the box.

D Complete the sentences with the words in the box.

expensive	hard	information	safe	wear

1. Don't play in the street! It isn't _____.
2. Ask your doctor for more _____.
3. Restaurants are _____, so we usually eat at home.
4. It's _____ for me to remember what to buy, so I make a shopping list.
5. When it rains, I _____ a raincoat.

E Complete the conversations with the words in the box.

anything	decide	price	worry

1. **A:** The _____ of gas is going up again.
   B: It's getting really expensive.
2. **A:** Can I have some cereal for a snack?
   B: You can have _____ you'd like.
3. **A:** Drive safely!
   B: I'll be fine. Don't _____ about me.
4. **A:** Where would you like to go for lunch?
   B: I don't know. I can't _____.

F Write *always*, *often*, and *usually* on the correct lines in the chart. Then circle the word in the sentence that is true for you.

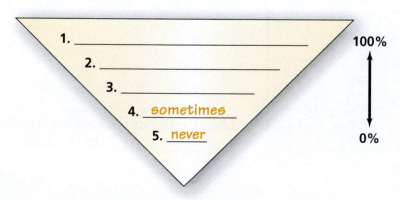

1. _____ 100%
2. _____
3. _____
4. _sometimes_
5. _never_ 0%

I (always / usually / often / sometimes / never) shop online.

DEVELOPING YOUR SKILLS

The Topic and the Main Idea

A Go back to page 97 and read "Online Shoppers" again.

B Answer the questions about the topic and the main idea of the reading.

1. What is the topic of the reading? Check (✓) your answer.
   - ☐ **a.** The Internet
   - ☐ **b.** Going shopping
   - ☐ **c.** People who shop online

2. What is the main idea of the reading? Check (✓) your answer.
   - ☐ **a.** Today, you can buy anything online.
   - ☐ **b.** There are different kinds of online shoppers.
   - ☐ **c.** Computers and the Internet are a great help to shoppers.

Reading for Details

  Read the definitions. Find the name for each group in the reading. Write it in the chart.

Groups of People	Definitions
1. online shoppers	people who use the Internet for shopping
2.	people who are new to online shopping
3.	people who love to find good prices
4.	people who shop online for fun
5.	people who shop online when they have to

B   **Read the questions. Circle the answer. Circle "It doesn't say" when the reading does not give that information.**

1. Do most people in the United States
   shop online?   Yes   No   (It doesn't say.)

2. Can someone buy a house online?   Yes   No   It doesn't say.

3. Can newcomers understand websites
   easily?   Yes   No   It doesn't say.

4. Are prices important to bargain hunters? Yes   No   It doesn't say.

5. Are older people usually bargain hunters? Yes   No   It doesn't say.

6. Are nonstop shoppers usually women?   Yes   No   It doesn't say.

7. Do single-minded shoppers like to spend
   a lot of time shopping online?   Yes   No   It doesn't say.

8. Do some shoppers worry about using
   their credit cards online?   Yes   No   It doesn't say.

Summarizing the Reading

Complete the summary of the reading on page 97. Use *feel*, *Internet*, *kinds*, *same*, and *shops*.

An online shopper is a person who _____ online. Online
                                          (1)
shoppers are not all the _____. Different _____ of
                              (2)   (3)
online shoppers use the _____ in different ways. Also, they do
                                (4)
not all _____ the same way about shopping online.
              (5)

Discussing the Reading

Talk about these questions with your class.

1. What is an online shopper?

2. How many kinds of online shoppers does the reading list? Name them.
   Tell something about each kind.

3. Think about online shoppers and in-store shoppers. How are they the
   same? How are they different?

4. Some people worry about shopping online. Why?

5. Do you shop online? What kind of online shopper are you?

Using New Words

Work alone or with a partner. Complete the sentences. Then copy your sentences on a piece of paper.

1. I **never** _____.
2. I **worry** about _____.
3. I think _____ can do **anything**.
4. I ask _____ when I need **information** about _____.
5. The **price** of _____ is _____.

Writing

Give one or more answers to each question. On a piece of paper, write your sentences in the form of a paragraph.

1. Do you have a computer at home?
2. Do you use the Internet?
3. Do you shop online?
4. Is shopping online a good idea?

Example:

I have a computer. I use the Internet every day. I sometimes shop online. I can get good prices online. I bought my new phone online. I think shopping online is a good idea.

CHAPTER 12

Returns and Exchanges

After shopping

Talk about these questions with your class.

1. Look at the photo. What do you see?

2. When you go shopping, how do you usually pay? Why?
   ☐ with cash
   ☐ with a personal check
   ☐ with a debit card
   ☐ with a credit card

3. The girl in the photo is looking at her **receipts**. What do you do with your receipts after you shop?
   ☐ I throw them in the trash.   ☐ I check the prices.
   ☐ I keep them.   ☐ other

Read to Find Out: What do shoppers need to know?

104

READING

Look at the words and picture next to the reading. Then read. Do not stop to use a dictionary.

Returns and Exchanges

1   Does this ever[1] happen to you? You buy something in a store. Then you get home, look at it again, and say, "Oh, no. This was a **mistake**." Maybe you think the price was **too** high. Maybe you bought[2] a shirt that does not really **fit**. Maybe you bought some food, and now you see that it is past its sell-by **date**.[3] What can you do about it?

2   In the United States, shoppers often take purchases[4] back to the store. Every year, they **return** more than one billion dollars in purchases.

3   When you return a purchase to a U.S. store, a salesperson will ask, "Do you have the receipt?" The receipt shows the name of the store. It also shows the date and price of the purchase. It is important not to **lose** the receipt. **If** you do not have it, the salesperson may say, "I'm sorry. I can't help you without a receipt."

4   If you have your receipt, sometimes you can get your money back. Sometimes a store will give you a store credit **only**. Store credit is like money, but you can spend it only in that store.

5   Maybe you like your purchase, but it is the **wrong** size. For example, you bought a jacket[5] in size 12, but you really need a 10. You can ask to make an exchange. An exchange means you give back your purchase and get the same thing in a different size or color.

6   Every store has different rules about returns and exchanges. You need to know the rules when you shop. Sometimes they are on your receipt. If they are, it is a good idea to read them before you **leave** the store.

[1] *ever* = at any time

[2] *bought* = the past of *buy*

[3] the *sell-by date* (for food) = the last day a store should sell the food

[4] a *purchase* = something you paid for

[5] a *jacket*

Quick Comprehension Check

A Read these sentences about the reading. Circle T (true) or F (false).

1. U.S. shoppers often take things back to the store.   T   F

2. Salespeople in U.S. stores have to give a shopper's
   money back.   T   F

3. Salespeople need to see a shopper's receipt.   T   F

4. The words *return*, *store credit*, and *exchange* all
   mean the same thing.   T   F

5. Shoppers need to know store rules about returns
   and exchanges.   T   F

B Can you answer the Read to Find Out question on page 104?

EXPLORING VOCABULARY

A Find the words in **bold** in "Returns and Exchanges" on page 105. Write
them in the list. Use alphabetical order.

1. date _____   6. _____

2. _____   7. _____

3. _____   8. _____

4. _____   9. _____

5. _____   10. _____

B Complete the sentences with the words in the box. The sentences are
about the reading.

date	if	leaves	lose	mistake	only	return

1. Sometimes, a shopper makes a _____. For example, a
   man at the supermarket thinks he sees *soup* on his list. He buys soup,
   but his wife did not want soup. She wanted soap.

2. There is sometimes a _____ written on a box or package
   of food. It shows the month, day, and year.

3. Sometimes shoppers take things back to the store. They
_____ them.

4. Remember to keep your receipts in a safe place. Don't
_____ them.

5. When U.S. shoppers do not have receipts, they usually cannot make
returns. _____ shoppers have receipts, then often they
can.

6. Sometimes a store will give just store credit. Shoppers cannot have
their money back. They can have _____ store credit.

7. After a customer finishes shopping, the customer _____
the store.

C Complete the sentences about the picture. Write *fit*, *too*, or *wrong*.

The sweater is _____ big for
the boy. It does not _____. It is
the _____ size for him.

D Complete the conversations with the words in the box.

if	leaving	lose	mistakes	too

1. **A:** Is Mike _____ home to go to college?
   B: Yes, he'll go next month.

2. **A:** Did you make many _____ on your test?
   B: No, I got 100%!

3. **A:** Are you going to buy that?
   B: I can't. It's _____ expensive.

4. **A:** Don't _____ your lunch money!
   B: Don't worry, Mom.

5. **A:** I'm not good at catching the ball.
   B: _____ you open your eyes, that will help!

E   **Match the words and their meanings. Write the letters.**

_____ 1. fit

_____ 2. date

_____ 3. only

_____ 4. return

_____ 5. wrong

a. just

b. not right, not correct

c. a day of the month or year

d. be the right size for someone

e. give something back, or go back

DEVELOPING YOUR SKILLS

The Topic and the Main Idea

A   **Go back to page 105 and read "Returns and Exchanges" again.**

B   **Answer the questions about the topic and the main idea of the reading.**

1. What is the topic of the reading? Check (✓) your answer.
   - ☐ a. Shopping mistakes
   - ☐ b. Talking to salespeople
   - ☐ c. Making returns and exchanges

2. What is the main idea of the reading? Check (✓) your answer.
   - ☐ a. Salespeople do not like to take things back from customers.
   - ☐ b. Shoppers need to know store rules about returns and exchanges.
   - ☐ c. You can always get your money back if you have your receipt.

Reading for Details

 A Read the definitions. Write *an exchange, a purchase, a receipt,* or *store credit.*

Words	Definitions
1.	a piece of paper showing that you paid for something
2.	something that you buy in a store
3.	something you get in a store and can use to buy things only in that store
4.	giving back one thing in a store and taking a different one

 B Read the questions about the reading. Circle the answer. Circle "It doesn't say" if the reading does not give that information.

1. Do U.S. shoppers sometimes return things to the store?   Yes   No   It doesn't say.

2. Does a box of food sometimes have a date on it?   Yes   No   It doesn't say.

3. Can shoppers always return clothes to U.S. stores?   Yes   No   It doesn't say.

4. Do salespeople usually ask to see a shopper's receipt?   Yes   No   It doesn't say.

5. Does a receipt show the date you were in a store?   Yes   No   It doesn't say.

6. Can you get your money back at most U.S. stores?   Yes   No   It doesn't say.

7. Do credit cards make it easy to return things to stores?   Yes   No   It doesn't say.

8. Do all stores have the same rules about returns and exchanges?   Yes   No   It doesn't say.

Summarizing the Reading

 A   Match the beginning and the end of each sentence.

_c_   **1.** Sometimes shoppers want to

____ **2.** Shoppers in the United States

____ **3.** Some U.S. stores give

____ **4.** Every store has

____ **5.** It is important for shoppers

a. different rules.

b. store credit only.

c. take a purchase back to the store.

d. to keep their receipts.

e. can often return or exchange purchases.

B   Copy the sentences. Write them as a paragraph on a piece of paper. You will have a summary of the reading.

Sometimes shoppers want to take a purchase back to the store. Shoppers in the United States . . .

Discussing the Reading

Talk about these questions with your class.

1. What is an example of a shopping mistake?
2. Do you ever buy the wrong thing when you shop for other people?
3. When would you return food to a supermarket?
4. Do you ever make returns or exchanges? Are they easy to do or not? Tell why.
5. Do stores in your home country have the same kinds of rules as U.S. stores?

Using New Words

Work alone or with a partner. Complete the sentences. Then copy your sentences on a piece of paper.

1. **If** I win a million dollars, I will _____.
2. I sometimes make **mistakes** when I _____.
3. I don't want to **lose** _____.
4. I worry about _____-ing the **wrong** _____.
5. It is not good to be **too** _____.

Writing

Answer the questions about something you are planning to buy. It can be something you want to buy today or at any time in the future. On a piece of paper, write your sentences in the form of a paragraph.

1. What are you planning to buy and why?

2. When and where are you planning to buy it?

Example:

I am planning to buy a winter jacket because the weather is getting cold. I don't have enough warm clothes. I want to go shopping this weekend, but I don't know where to go. Can you tell me?

Wrap-up

REVIEWING VOCABULARY

Circle the correct word to complete the sentence.

1. She can't help us. She's _____ busy.
   a. too   **b.** hard   **c.** wrong

2. I can give you money _____ you need some.
   a. almost   **b.** if   **c.** only

3. If I get a great job, maybe I will _____ and I can buy a big house.
   a. keep   **b.** worry   **c.** get rich

4. We often make _____ when we are learning a new language.
   a. prices   **b.** mistakes   **c.** reports

5. This jacket is too big. It does not _____ me.
   a. wear   **b.** own   **c.** fit

6. You can go online to get _____ about many things.
   a. information   **b.** salespeople   **c.** safe

7. Keep your money in a safe place. Don't _____ it.
   a. understand   **b.** return   **c.** lose

8. I want a new TV, _____ I am going to the store to buy one.
   a. anything   **b.** so   **c.** usually

9. Rich people often wear _____ clothes.
   a. nothing   **b.** expensive   **c.** almost

10. He _____ his office at 5:30 and goes home.
    a. leaves   **b.** decides   **c.** keeps

EXPANDING VOCABULARY

Verbs

There are many different kinds of words. A noun is one kind of word. You learned about nouns on page 82.

A **verb** is a kind of word, too. Every sentence needs a verb.

What Is a Verb?		Examples of Verbs
A verb is a word for	an action:	*buy, drive, go, run, talk, write*
	a feeling or an experience:	*be, feel, know, like, seem, think, want*

A verb can have many forms: *talk*, *talks*, and *talked*, for example.

A verb can also have more than one part: *don't talk*, *is talking*, and *can talk*, for example.

Each sentence has one verb. Find and circle the verb.

1. (Catch) the ball!
2. I often use the Internet.
3. He never wears a hat.
4. Children grow quickly.
5. My mother enjoys love stories.
6. I agree with you.
7. They own a small boat.
8. I am returning this jacket.
9. I don't understand the homework.
10. They can't decide on a name for the baby.
11. Fruit is a good snack.
12. Please remember the date.

A PUZZLE

Complete the sentences and the puzzle. Look at the word lists on pages 90, 98, and 106 for help.

Across

3. I can't w_____ these shoes. They are too big.

6. They o_____ a small house.

8. The p_____ for that car is more than $50,000.

10. It o_____ rains at this time of year.

12. If you have questions, ask your doctor for i_____.

13. It u_____ does not get very cold in Florida.

Down

1. If you have the receipt, you can return_____ that shirt to the store.

2. I tried to call you, but I had the w_____ number.

4. She is a great cook. She can cook a_____.

5. Some people w_____ about flying, but I think it's safe.

7. There is a r_____ on the fire in the newspaper today.

9. Is it a_____ time for lunch? I'm getting hungry.

11. I can't buy this shirt. It's $32 and I have o_____ $25.

EXTRA READING

Gift Cards

1   A gift is something that you give to someone. For example, flowers are a nice gift for a mother on Mother's Day. Many of us enjoy giving gifts, but sometimes it is hard to think of the right gift for someone. What will make the person happy?

2   Many U.S. stores say: "Here's an idea. Buy a gift card!" A gift card looks something like a credit card. It is usually the same size. You pay for it at the store or buy it online. You spend the amount[1] you want: $10, $25, $50, or more. Then you give the card to someone as a gift. That person can take it to the store and spend it on anything he or she likes.

[1] *amount* = how much there is of something

3   Different stores have different rules for their gift cards. For example, some cards have an expiration date. An expiration date means the card is no good after that date. Also, for some cards, there are fees.[2] If you wait a year to use a $50 gift card, it may be good for only $44. That is because of the fees.

[2] a *fee* = money you pay to use or do something

4   If you get a gift card, keep it in a safe place. It is just like money. If you lose it, the store will not give you a new one.

5   A gift card can be a nice idea when you cannot think of anything to give. Just remember to ask about the rules before you buy it.

Comprehension Check

Read these sentences about the reading. Circle T (true) or F (false).

1. Gifts are things that we give to people.   T   F

2. A gift card is the same as a credit card.   T   F

3. You can buy gift cards only in stores.   T   F

4. First, you use a gift card; then you pay for it later.   T   F

5. Every store has rules for its gift cards.   T   F

Reading for Details

Read the questions. Circle the answer. Circle "It doesn't say" if the reading does not give that information.

1. Are flowers an example of a gift?   Yes   No   It doesn't say.

2. Do most people in the United States give flowers on Mother's Day?   Yes   No   It doesn't say.

3. Do many stores in the United States sell gift cards?   Yes   No   It doesn't say.

4. Is a gift card a kind of credit card?   Yes   No   It doesn't say.

5. Do gift cards usually look a little like credit cards?   Yes   No   It doesn't say.

6. Is the expiration date on the back of the card?   Yes   No   It doesn't say.

7. Do teenagers love to buy things with gift cards?   Yes   No   It doesn't say.

The Topic and the Main Idea

1. What is the topic of the reading? Check (✓) your answer.
   - ☐ **a.** Gifts for family and friends
   - ☐ **b.** Rules for giving gifts
   - ☐ **c.** Gift cards

2. What is the main idea of the reading? Check (✓) your answer.
   - ☐ **a.** Gift cards can be nice gifts, but you need to know the gift card rules.
   - ☐ **b.** Sometimes it is not easy to think of the right gifts for family or friends.
   - ☐ **c.** A gift card is easy to buy, easy to use, and easy to lose.

Vocabulary Self-Test 2

Choose an answer to complete each sentence. Circle the letter of your answer.

Example:

Breakfast is my favorite _____ of the day.

   a. box   **b.** meal   **c.** lunch

1. You have to run to _____ the ball.

   a. understand   **b.** catch   **c.** wear

2. There is a lot of _____ on the Internet.

   a. return   **b.** together   **c.** information

3. Call me _____ you need anything.

   a. without   **b.** if   **c.** often

4. _____ player wears a different number.

   a. Both   **b.** Rich   **c.** Each

5. China has more people than any other country in the _____.

   a. field   **b.** world   **c.** date

6. Please _____ not to laugh!

   a. try   **b.** beat   **c.** hold

7. They have flowers all _____ their house.

   a. around   **b.** usually   **c.** too

8. No, this isn't 555-2000; you have the _____ number.

   a. wrong   **b.** safe   **c.** only

9. I always learn a lot when I read his _____.

   a. teams   **b.** reports   **c.** prices

10. That _____ expensive to me. What do you think?

   a. keeps   **b.** leaves   **c.** seems

11. We need to _____ what to do about this problem.

    a. decide   **b.** enjoy   **c.** pick up

12. He doesn't _____ a car and doesn't want to.

    a. laugh   **b.** own   **c.** agree

13. I do crossword puzzles in pencil, not pen, because I make many _____.

    a. salespeople   **b.** rules   **c.** mistakes

14. I'm sorry, but I don't _____ your name.

    a. keep   **b.** collect   **c.** remember

15. Mothers and fathers often _____ about their children.

    a. lose   **b.** fit   **c.** worry

16. That store is closed, _____ we can't shop there.

    a. almost   **b.** so   **c.** if

17. We're sorry, but there is _____ we can do.

    a. nothing   **b.** expensive   **c.** hard

18. We need two people to _____ the TV.

    a. carry   **b.** hope   **c.** happen

See the Answer Key on page 150.

UNIT
5

ON THE JOB

Working Teens

Teens[1] at work

GETTING READY TO READ

Talk about these questions with your class.

1. Look at the photos. What do you see?
2. What kinds of jobs do high school students do? List some jobs or some places where they often work.
3. What do you think: What is a good age to start working?

[1] a *teen* = a teenager, a person who is 13–19 years old

READ TO FIND OUT: When do U.S. teens usually start working?

READING

Look at the words next to the reading. Then read. Do not stop to use a dictionary.

Working Teens

1   Is it a good idea for teenagers to work before they finish high school? Some people say yes, teens **should** work. Others say no, they should not. **Let's** listen to a few **opinions**:

Jeff Baker, father: Teenagers are expensive! I want my kid[1] to get a job.

Wendy Tajima, mother: I think kids today work too much.

Don Robbins, teacher: High school students should be studying, not working.

April Baker, teenager: It's my **life**! I'll work if I want to!

[1] *my kid* = my son or daughter

2   Let's look at some **facts** about working teens in the United States. Many U.S. high school students have jobs. More than **half** of all U.S. teens start working before they are 15 years old. Some work only in the summer, but most work **during** the school year, too. Some high school students work full-time.[2]

[2] *full-time* = 35 or more hours a week

3   There are good **reasons** for teenagers to work. They can learn things on the job that they cannot learn in school. Making money feels good, too. Some teenagers use the money to help their **parents**.

4   There are also good reasons for them not to work. Working takes time. Teens may need that time to do schoolwork and to get enough sleep. They also need time to build relationships.[3] The fact is, studies[4] show that more than 20 hours' work a week is bad for teens. It is bad for their schoolwork and for relationships **between** teens and their families and friends.

[3] *a relationship* = the connection between two people

[4] *studies* = work done to learn something and then written about in reports

5   Maybe you can think of more reasons why high school students should or should not work. What is your opinion on the question?

Quick Comprehension Check

A **Read these sentences about the reading. Circle T (true) or F (false).**

1. A lot of high school students in the United States   T   F
   have jobs.

2. Everyone in the United States thinks work is good   T   F
   for teenagers.

3. U.S. teens usually start work when they are 16 or   T   F
   older.

4. Teenagers can help their families by working.   T   F

5. Working can be a bad idea for teenagers.   T   F

B **Can you answer the Read to Find Out question on page 120?**

EXPLORING VOCABULARY

A **Find the words in bold in "Working Teens" on page 121. Write them in the list. Use alphabetical order.**

1. between _____   6. _____

2. _____   7. _____

3. _____   8. _____

4. _____   9. _____

5. _____   10. _____

B **Complete the sentences with the words in the box. The sentences are about the reading.**

| during | fact | let's | life | opinions | reasons | should |

1. Some people think it is good for teenagers to have jobs. They think
   teenagers _____ work.

2. Use "_____ go" when you mean "I want us to go
   together."

3. People do not all think the same way about jobs for teenagers. People have different _____—different ideas or ways of thinking. They do not all agree.

4. The time that you live, from the beginning to the end, is your

   _____.

5. Many U.S. high school students work. That is a _____. That is a piece of information that is true.

6. Most U.S. teenagers with jobs work _____ the school year—from September to June—not just in the summer.

7. Why should teenagers work? The reading gives some answers to this question. It gives a few _____ why working is good for teens.

C **Complete the sentences about the pictures. Write** *between*, *half*, **or** *parents*.

1. Would you like _____ of my apple?

2. That's me, and those are my _____.

3. The post office is _____ the bank and the police station.

D Complete the sentences with the words in the box.

during	facts	half	lives	parents	should

1. Please do not use your cell phone _____ class.
2. Do you look like your _____ ?
3. The children seem to be learning a lot of _____ about the sun.
4. Almost _____ of the students work: 11 out of 24 have jobs.
5. We really _____ thank him for his help.
6. Some people spend half their _____ doing jobs they don't enjoy.

E Complete the conversations with the words in the box.

between	let's	opinion	reason

1. **A:** Doctor, will my father be OK?
   B: Yes, there's no _____ for you to worry.
2. **A:** I need to learn to use all these new words.
   B: So do I. _____ practice them together.
3. **A:** Well, in my _____, she shouldn't be out after 10:00 P.M.
   B: I agree.
4. **A:** Do you want to get something to eat _____ classes?
   B: Yeah, let's do that. I'm free from 11:00 to 12:00. How about you?

DEVELOPING YOUR SKILLS

The Topic and the Main Idea

A Go back to page 121 and read "Working Teens" again.

B Answer the questions about the topic and the main idea of the reading.

1. What is the topic of the reading? Check (✓) your answer.
    - ☐ **a.** High school students and work
    - ☐ **b.** Teenagers and money
    - ☐ **c.** Good jobs for teens

2. What is another good title for the reading? Choose the title that gives the main idea. Check (✓) your answer.
    - ☐ **a.** Should High School Students Have Jobs?
    - ☐ **b.** How Much Do Teenagers Work?
    - ☐ **c.** Who Wants Teens to Work?

Scanning the Reading

A Scan the reading on page 121. Find the words to complete the sentences.

1. People have different _____ about teens and work.
2. Many _____ students in the United States have jobs.
3. More than 50 percent of all U.S. teenagers start working before they are _____ years old.
4. Most teens with jobs work in the summer and during _____, too.
5. There are good _____ for teenagers to work—and for them not to work, too.
6. Studies show that teens should not work more than _____ hours a week during the school year.

B   **Complete the chart. Use information from the reading.**

Reasons for High School Students to Work	Reasons for High School Students Not to Work
1.	1.
2.	2.
3.	3.

Fact vs. Opinion

Does each sentence state a fact or give an opinion? Write *fact* or *opinion* on the line.

1. Teenagers are expensive.   *opinion*

2. Many U.S. high school students have jobs.   *fact*

3. High school students should not work.   _____

4. Some teens work only in the summer.   _____

5. Some teens make money to help their families.   _____

6. High school students do not study enough.   _____

7. Teens cannot get enough sleep if they work.   _____

8. Studies show that working can be bad for teens.   _____

Discussing the Reading

Do you agree or disagree with each opinion? Check (✓) your answers. Talk with your class about the reasons for your answers.

Opinions	I agree.	I disagree.
1. Teenagers are expensive for their parents.	☐	☐
2. It is good for high school students to work.	☐	☐
3. Some things are more important than work for teenagers.	☐	☐
4. Teenagers should decide when and if they will work.	☐	☐

Using New Words

Work alone or with a partner. Complete the sentences. Then copy your sentences on a piece of paper.

1. I would like to _____ every day **during** the summer.

2. One of the most important things in my **life** is

    _____.

3. A good **parent** _____.

4. _____ is **between** _____ and

    _____.

5. Let's _____.

Writing

On a piece of paper, write about high school students and work. Give your opinion and your reasons for it. You can begin:

In my opinion, it (is / is not) a good idea for high school students to work.

Example:

   In my opinion, it is a good idea for high school students to work. It is good because they can get experience. They can learn something. It is not good for them to work full-time because . . .

Night Work

*Construction workers
on the night shift*

GETTING READY TO READ

Talk about these questions with your class.

1. Look at the photo. What do you see?

2. What hours do most people work?

3. What time of day or night do you like to go to sleep?

4. An owl is a kind of bird. Some people are called "night owls." What do you think that means?

READ TO FIND OUT: What is a night owl?

READING

Look at the words and pictures next to the reading. Then read. Do not stop to use a dictionary.

Night Work

1 Most of us work during the day and sleep at night, but not everyone does. Some people work at night. In the United States, for example, there are more than 20 million[1] night workers.

2 We need night workers in our 24/7 world, but working at night may be bad for the people who do it. Here are three reasons to worry about working at night.

3 • Many night workers do not sleep well during the day. They feel tired at night, so they make mistakes, and they **forget** things. Night workers have more **accidents**, too. If they work with **machines**, they can **get hurt**.

4 • Night workers have to eat, but our **bodies** are made for eating during the day, not at night. People are not like bats![2] Eating at night can give a person problems with his or her digestive system.[3]

5 • Night workers often do not see much of their friends and families. Working the night **shift** sometimes means husbands and wives do not have enough time together. It can make life **difficult**. Many U.S. night workers get divorced.[4]

6 With all these problems, why do people work at night? Some people do it to make more money. Some do it to be home with their children during the day. Some do it because they are happier doing things at night. These people are called "night owls."

7 Donna Smith is a night owl. She loves working the night shift at her **company**. She starts work at 9:00 P.M. and leaves for home at 6:00 A.M. Donna says, "Working the night shift is great. All the bosses[5] are home in bed. We work **hard** but without the **stress**."

[1] *20 million =* 20,000,000

[2] a *bat*

[3] the *digestive system*

[4] *get divorced* = stop being married

[5] the *boss* = the person who tells workers what to do

Quick Comprehension Check

A   **Read these sentences about the reading. Circle T (true) or F (false).**

1. Many U.S. workers work at night and sleep during the day.   T   F

2. The reading says working at night is good for you.   T   F

3. Night workers sometimes make mistakes because they are tired.   T   F

4. Night work can make life hard for married people.   T   F

5. Night owls are people who sleep well at night.   T   F

B   **Can you answer the Read to Find Out question on page 128?**

EXPLORING VOCABULARY

A   **Find the words in bold in "Night Work" on page 129. Write them in the list. Use alphabetical order.**

1. accidents _____   6. _____

2. _____   7. _____

3. _____   8. _____

4. _____   9. _____

5. _____   10. _____

B   **Complete the sentences with the words in the box. The sentences are about the reading.**

| company | difficult | forget | hard | hurt | shift | stress |

1. It's hard to remember things if you don't get enough sleep. When night workers are tired, they _____ things.

2. If someone is working with a machine and makes a mistake, bad things can happen. People can get _____.

3. A _____ is the hours that a group of workers are on the job. For example, *first shift* may be from 7:00 A.M. to 3:00 P.M.

4. It can be hard to have your husband or wife working nights. It can make married life _____.

5. Donna Smith works for a _____. She works for a business that makes or sells something.

6. Donna doesn't sleep on the job. She works _____. She tries to do her job well.

7. Many workers don't like to work with the boss watching. It makes them worry. They feel _____.

C **Complete the sentences about the pictures. Write *accident*, *body*, or *machine*.**

1. This is a sewing _____.

2. George had a car _____.

arm

3. How many parts of the _____ can you name?

D Complete the sentences with the words in the box.

body	difficult	machines	shift	stress

1. Cars, computers, and airplanes are all _____.
2. Your head, hands, legs, and feet are all parts of your

   _____.
3. In my opinion, it's _____ to learn a new language.
4. Yuri works the night _____ at the hospital, so he starts at
   11:00 P.M.
5. When I think about everything I have to do, I feel a lot of

   _____.

E Complete the conversations with the words in the box.

accident	company	forget	hard	hurt

1. **A:** That's a big bicycle for a little boy.

   B: I know. I'm afraid he'll get _____.

2. **A:** What _____ does she work for?

   B: Apple. They make computers.

3. **A:** Don't _____: There's no class on Friday.

   B: Don't worry, I'll remember!

4. **A:** She says she isn't doing well in school.

   B: I think she's just not trying _____ enough.

5. **A:** What happened?

   B: It was an _____.

DEVELOPING YOUR SKILLS

The Topic and the Main Idea

A Go back to page 129 and read "Night Work" again.

B Answer the questions about the topic and the main idea of the reading.

1. What is the topic of the reading? Check (✓) your answer.
   - ☐ **a.** Reasons we need night workers
   - ☐ **b.** Different kinds of night work
   - ☐ **c.** People who work at night

2. What is another good title for the reading? Choose the title that gives the main idea. Check (✓) your answer.
   - ☐ **a.** How to Find a Good Night Job
   - ☐ **b.** Five Good Reasons to Work at Night
   - ☐ **c.** A Few Facts about Working at Night

Reading for Details

A Complete the answers to the questions.

1. How many night workers are there in the United States? There are

   _____.

2. Who is Donna Smith? She is _____.

3. When does Donna Smith work? She works

   _____.

4. Why does she work at night? She is _____.

5. Who is "home in bed" at night? _____ are.

B   **Complete the chart. Use information from the reading.**

Reasons Some People Work at Night	Reasons Not to Work at Night
1.	1.
2.	2.
3.	3.

Fact vs. Opinion

Does each sentence state a fact or give an opinion? Write *fact* or *opinion* on the line.

1. Working at night is fun. _____opinion_____

2. Millions of Americans work at night. _____fact_____

3. Most people work during the day. _____

4. Some people work at night to make more money. _____

5. Night owls are often happy doing things at night. _____

6. Working the night shift is easy. _____

7. Night workers feel more stress than other people. _____

8. Working at night is a bad idea. _____

Discussing the Reading

Talk about these questions with your class.

1. The reading says, "We need night workers in our 24/7 world." What does "our 24/7 world" mean? List some examples of night workers we need.

2. How can working at night be bad for a person?

3. Why do some people work at night?

4. Are you a morning person or a night owl? Tell why.

Using New Words

Work alone or with a partner. Complete the sentences. Then copy your sentences on a piece of paper.

1. It's **difficult** for me to _____.
2. People have **accidents** when they _____.
3. I sometimes **forget** _____.
4. You can **get hurt** if you _____.
5. I feel **stress** when _____.

Writing

Think about your answers to the questions. Then write a short paragraph with your answers on a piece of paper.

1. Are you a morning person or a night owl?
2. Do you like to go to bed early or stay up late?
3. Do you like to get up early or sleep late?
4. What is your favorite time of day or night to do homework?

Example:

I am a morning person. I like to go to bed early. I usually go to bed at 9:30 P.M. I like to get up early, too. My favorite time to do homework is . . .

Working for Tips

Picting up a tip

GETTING READY TO READ

Talk about these questions with your class.

1. Look at the photo. What is happening?

2. Read the definition of the word *tip*. Then check (✓) all the people who get tips.

   tip *n.* an amount of money that you give to someone who does a service for you, for example, a . . .

   ☐ waiter   ☐ bus driver

   ☐ teacher   ☐ pizza delivery person

   ☐ taxi driver   ☐ salesperson

   READ TO FIND OUT: Do people in the United States agree on rules for tipping?

Look at the words next to the reading. Then read. Do not stop to use a dictionary.

Working for Tips

1   David Vargas is a waiter. He works at a nice restaurant in a **large** U.S. city. The minimum wage there is **over** $8.00 an hour. That means all workers in the state[1] should get more than $8.00 an hour. David does not. He gets only $4.23 an hour from his employer.[2] That is because waiters get tips.

2   In many countries, people do not give tips. Workers there do not **expect** tips. In the United States, people often give tips. They expect to tip waiters and taxi drivers, for example. Waiters and taxi drivers expect to get tips. In fact, most of their pay comes from tips.

3   David says, "A **fair** tip for a server[3] is 15 percent[4] of your **bill**. If a server does a really good job for you, give 20 percent. But if you are with a group of people, look at your bill. Maybe the tip is on it. Some restaurants put the tip for a large group on the bill."

4   You can find rules for tipping on the Internet, but not everyone agrees on them. Some people **believe** tipping is wrong. Here are a few comments[5] from one website:

From Gary in Ohio: Why should I give a bigger tip on a $30 meal than on a $20 meal? The waiter doesn't work more!

From Rudy in California: I tip the pizza delivery kid[6] 50¢. He's just a kid.

From Fran in Georgia: I don't believe in tipping. It makes me **angry**. People should just do their jobs and not expect extra money.

5   What does David think about these comments? He says, "These people don't work for tips. They don't understand. Maybe things will **change** in the **future**, but that's not going to happen **soon**. And for now, people like me really need our tips."

---

[1] a *state* = one of the 50 parts of the United States, such as Texas or Florida

[2] *his employer* = the person or company that pays him to work

[3] *server* = another word for *waiter*

[4] *percent* = %

[5] a *comment* = an opinion someone says or writes

[6] a *kid* = a young person

Quick Comprehension Check

A   **Read these sentences about the reading. Circle T (true) or F (false).**

1. David Vargas owns a restaurant.   T   F

2. Waiters in U.S. restaurants usually get tips.   T   F

3. David thinks tipping is a bad idea.   T   F

4. David thinks tips are not really important.   T   F

5. You can read about tipping on the Internet.   T   F

B   **Can you answer the Read to Find Out question on page 136?**

EXPLORING VOCABULARY

A   **Find the words in bold in "Working for Tips" on page 137. Write them in the list. Use alphabetical order.**

1. angry
2. _____
3. _____
4. _____
5. _____

6. _____
7. _____
8. _____
9. _____
10. _____

B   **Complete the sentences with the words in the box. The sentences are about the reading.**

believe	bill	change	expect	future	over	soon

1. If a worker gets _____ $8.00 an hour, that means he or she gets more than $8.00 an hour.

2. Waiters and taxi drivers in the United States _____ tips. They think they will get tips.

3. At the end of a meal in a restaurant, the waiter brings the
_____ (or *the check*). This paper tells how much you have
to pay.

4. Some people think tipping is a good idea. Other people
_____ it is not.

5. Some things are always the same, but some things are not. They
_____.

6. The time we are in now is the present. The time that is coming is the
_____.

7. David says tipping rules may change. If they change, it will happen
far in the future. It will not happen _____.

C Complete the sentences about the pictures. Write *angry*, *fair*, or *large*.

Sam is _____. His ice cream cone
(1)

is small, but his brother's is _____.
(2)

Sam says, "It's not _____!"
(3)

D What is the meaning of each word in **bold** letters? Circle *a*, *b*, or *c*.

1. I'd like a **large** glass of water, please.

   a. big   **b.** difficult   **c.** wrong

2. I **expect** this shirt will fit my son.

   a. want   **b.** forget   **c.** think

    (it to happen)   (it happened)   (it will happen)

3. There are **over** 500 people working for the company.

   a. too much   **b.** more than   **c.** half of

4. I **believe** he works the night shift at the hospital.

   a. hope   **b.** think   **c.** know

5. Let's get together again **soon**.

   a. never   **b.** often   **c.** in the near future

E **Complete the conversations with the words in the box.**

angry	bill	change	fair	future

1. **A:** How much is the phone _____ this month?

   B: Over $50.

2. **A:** You should tell your parents about the accident.

   B: But I'm afraid they'll be _____ with me.

3. **A:** In the _____, he hopes to have a job with good pay and no stress.

   B: A hard job to find, I believe.

4. **A:** I cooked, so you wash the dishes, OK?

   B: OK, that's _____.

5. **A:** Do you like going back home for visits?

   B: Yes, nothing ever seems to _____ there.

DEVELOPING YOUR SKILLS

The Topic and the Main Idea

A **Go back to page 137 and read "Working for Tips" again.**

B **Answer the questions about the topic and the main idea of the reading.**

1. What is the topic of the reading? Check (✓) your answer.

   ☐ **a.** Being a waiter

   ☐ **b.** New rules for tipping

   ☐ **c.** Giving and getting tips

2. What is another good title for the reading? Choose the title that gives the main idea. Check (✓) your answer.

   ☐ **a.** A Day in the Life of a Waiter

   ☐ **b.** Changing the Rules for Tipping

   ☐ **c.** Facts and Opinions about Tipping

Reading for Details

A **Complete the answers to the questions.**

1. What does David Vargas do for a living? He is a _____.

2. How much does David get paid? He gets _____ an hour plus tips.

3. Who expects tips in the United States? Waiters and _____ are two examples.

4. When do some restaurants put the tip on the bill? They do it when there is a large _____ of people.

5. Where can you read opinions about tipping? You can find comments _____.

6. Who thinks tipping is not going to change any time soon? _____ does.

B **Whose opinion is it? Write David, Gary, Rudy, or Fran.**

Opinion	Speaker
1. A fair tip for a server is 15–20% of the bill.	David
2. A waiter doesn't work more to bring me a $30 meal than a $20 meal, so why should I tip more?	
3. People shouldn't expect tips just for doing their jobs.	
4. People who work for tips need the money.	
5. Kids don't need big tips.	

Summarizing the Reading

Complete the summary of the reading. Use agrees, believe, bill, example, expect, and fair.

Some workers in the United States _____ tips: waiters
(1)

and taxi drivers, for _____. David Vargas is a waiter who
(2)

says 15 to 20 percent of the _____ is a _____
(3)   (4)

tip. Not everyone _____ about giving tips. Some people
(5)

_____ they should not have to give tips.
(6)

Discussing the Reading

Talk about these questions with your class.

1. David Vargas does not get paid the minimum wage in his state. Why not?
2. What examples of people who work for tips does the reading give? What other examples can you give?
3. What different opinions on tipping do people give in the reading?
4. What is your opinion about giving tips?

Using New Words

Work alone or with a partner. Complete the sentences. Then copy your sentences on a piece of paper.

1. People often get **angry** when _____.
2. I have to pay my _____ **bill**.
3. I have to pay **over** _____ for _____.
4. I'm going to _____ sometime **soon**.
5. In the **future**, I hope _____.

Writing

On a piece of paper, write about giving or working for tips. Give your opinion and your reasons for it. You can begin:

In my opinion, it (is / is not) a good idea to (give / work for) tips.

Example:

In my opinion, it is a good idea to give tips. If somebody does a good job, you give a good tip. If somebody doesn't do a good job, you don't. I think people try hard to do a good job and get a good tip.

REVIEWING VOCABULARY

Circle the correct word to complete the sentence.

1. It takes _____ five hours to get there by car.
   a. soon   **b.** over   **c.** between

2. Let's not talk _____ the movie.
   a. between   **b.** hard   **c.** during

3. Yes, I remember him but I _____ his name.
   a. hurt   **b.** forget   **c.** expect

4. There's nothing to get _____ about.
   a. bill   **b.** angry   **c.** large

5. I expect it to be the happiest day of my _____.
   a. fact   **b.** body   **c.** life

6. If you wash _____ the dishes, I'll finish them.
   a. half   **b.** fair   **c.** shift

7. I'm feeling a lot of _____ because I have a lot of schoolwork.
   a. opinion   **b.** reason   **c.** stress

8. I hope this cold, rainy weather will _____ soon.
   a. change   **b.** believe   **c.** future

EXPANDING VOCABULARY

Adjectives

There are many different kinds of words. You learned about nouns on page 82 and verbs on page 113.

An **adjective** is a kind of word, too. Adjectives describe people, places, things, and ideas.

Rules for Adjectives in Sentences	Examples			
1. Use adjective + noun.			Adjective	Noun
	They have a		**big**	house.
			beautiful	daughter.
			new	plan.
2. Use the verb *be*, *get*, or *seem* + adjective.		*Be/Get/Seem*	Adjective	
	That answer	is	**wrong**.	
	I	'm getting	**ready**	to leave.
	He	doesn't seem	**angry**.	

Each sentence has one adjective. Find and circle the adjective.

1. I need some (extra) practice.

2. You seem tired.

3. That isn't fair!

4. Who is your favorite actor?

5. It's a difficult job.

6. Keep the receipt in a safe place.

7. I hope you'll get rich.

8. We're studying different kinds of words.

9. That large box is for you.

10. Will the test be hard?

A PUZZLE

Complete the sentences and the puzzle. Look at the word lists on pages 122, 130, and 138 for help.

Across

3. He works with a m_____ that makes boxes.

4. The police are asking for information about the a_____.

5. In my o_____, that's a very bad idea.

8. There's no r_____ to be afraid.

11. Is that a f_____ or just your opinion?

12. In the f_____, we won't make that mistake.

Down

1. I know I can catch the ball if I try _____hard_____ enough.

2. A snack is something you eat b_____ meals.

6. Where are the child's p_____?

7. *Toyota* is the name of a Japanese c_____.

9. Everyone s_____ eat a good breakfast.

10. Russia is a very l_____ country.

Help for Working Parents

1   Olivia and Michael are under a lot of stress. Olivia works over 40 hours a week. Michael does, too. They do not have enough time with their children. They do not see enough of their aging[1] parents.

2   Many working men and women have the same problem. They spend too much time at work. They feel they cannot be good parents. "What kind of life is this?" they ask. Many say, "Something has to change!"

3   In fact, things are changing. Many companies are trying to be more family-friendly.[2] They are making changes in the workplace. Here are three examples:

4   • Some companies have flextime. This means workers can change the hours they work. Some workers come in early and leave early. Others work two long days and three short days.

5   • Some companies let[3] people work at home part of the time. More than half of all U.S. companies with over 100 workers do this. The workers use computers and telephones at home to do their jobs.

6   • Some companies let workers job-share. Job-sharing means two workers do one job. Each worker does half the work and gets half the pay.

7   Employers[4] know that tired and unhappy workers cannot do a great job. Many employers are ready to change. It is not just good for their workers. It is good for the company, too.

[1] *aging* = growing old

[2] *family-friendly* = helping people both work and have a family life

[3] *let* = say something is OK to do, permit

[4] an *employer* = a person or company that pays a worker

Comprehension Check

Read these sentences about the reading. Circle T (true) or F (false).

1. Many working parents are under stress.   T   F

2. Companies are asking workers not to have children.   T   F

3. Companies cannot change their rules to help workers.　　　T　　F

4. Some U.S. companies let people work at home.　　　T　　F

5. Companies are changing to be more family-friendly.　　　T　　F

Reading for Details

Complete these statements about the reading.

1. Olivia works _____ hours a week.

2. Olivia and Michael want more time with _____.

3. A lot of companies want to be more _____.

4. "_____" means workers can change the hours they work.

5. Some companies let workers work _____ part of the time.

6. "_____" means two workers do one job.

Fact vs. Opinion

Does each sentence state a fact or give an opinion? Write *fact* or *opinion* on the line.

1. Michael works more than 40 hours a week.　　　_____fact_____

2. Men who work a lot are not good fathers.　　　_____

3. The reading gives three examples of changes in the workplace.　　　_____

4. More companies should have flextime.　　　_____

5. Many large U.S. companies let workers work at home.　　　_____

6. Job-sharing is a great idea.　　　_____

The Main Idea

Choose another title for the reading. Choose the title that gives the main idea. Check (✓) your answer.

☐ **a.** One Family's Problem

☐ **b.** Family-Friendly Changes in the Workplace

☐ **c.** The Future of Workers in the United States

Vocabulary Self-Test 3

Choose an answer to complete each sentence. Circle the letter of your answer.

Example:

Breakfast is my favorite _____ of the day.

a. box   **b.** meal   **c.** lunch   **d.** report

1. We expect newspapers to give us _____.

 a. parents   **b.** facts   **c.** meals   **d.** snacks

2. _____ play Rock, Paper, Scissors!

 a. Maybe   **b.** Only   **c.** Let's   **d.** Would like

3. Don't worry. They'll be home _____.

 a. usually   **b.** soon   **c.** hurt   **d.** difficult

4. She's rich, so she can buy _____.

 a. anything   **b.** nothing   **c.** just   **d.** other

5. I can't _____ the word.

 a. carry   **b.** remember   **c.** agree   **d.** hope

6. If you cut something in _____, you have two pieces.

 a. half   **b.** kind   **c.** size   **d.** company

7. Everyone _____ wash their hands before eating.

 a. almost   **b.** should   **c.** too   **d.** use

8. I'm afraid of _____ drivers!

 a. fair   **b.** favorite   **c.** safe   **d.** angry

9. I enjoy going to the movies with _____ friends.

 a. the wrong   **b.** each   **c.** a few   **d.** also

10. Help! Our group is having _____, and we don't know what to do.

 a. problems   **b.** details   **c.** examples   **d.** bodies

11. I hope they will have a happy _____ together.

 a. bill   **b.** field   **c.** price   **d.** life

12. People's opinions can _____.

    a. change   **b.** return   **c.** spend   **d.** forget

13. He works _____ the day and goes to classes in the evening.

    a. because   **b.** over   **c.** between   **d.** during

14. They're a good team. They play _____ together.

    a. every   **b.** ready   **c.** well   **d.** tired

15. In my _____, you should get more information before you decide.

    a. bowl   **b.** opinion   **c.** machine   **d.** laugh

16. I _____ that is true, but I don't really know.

    a. happen   **b.** may   **c.** believe   **d.** wear

17. It won't fit in the car. It's _____ big.

    a. enough   **b.** more   **c.** around   **d.** too

18. What does this word _____?

    a. mean   **b.** grow   **c.** keep   **d.** own

19. Give me one good _____ why I should listen to him!

    a. reason   **b.** box   **c.** mistake   **d.** shift

20. Most teachers _____ students to do homework.

    a. smell   **b.** beat   **c.** expect   **d.** collect

21. The players work _____ at practice.

    a. without   **b.** expensive   **c.** busy   **d.** hard

22. Please _____ the door open.

    a. lose   **b.** hold   **c.** seem   **d.** learn

23. He _____ spending time online.

    a. enjoys   **b.** catches   **c.** picks up   **d.** leaves

24. The parents of a new baby may be under a lot of _____.

    a. rules   **b.** expensive   **c.** stress   **d.** lunch

25. We hope to see you more often in the _____.

    a. date   **b.** accident   **c.** report   **d.** future

See the Answer Key on page 150.

VOCABULARY SELF-TESTS ANSWER KEY

Here are the answers to the Vocabulary Self-Tests. Check your answers. Then study any words you did not remember. Look for the words in the Index to Target Vocabulary on page 151. Then go back to the readings and exercises with the words. Use your dictionary as needed.

Vocabulary Self-Test 1 (Units 1–2, pages 57–58)

1. c. practice
2. b. size
3. c. extra
4. a. most
5. b. snack
6. a. mean
7. a. other
8. b. too
9. b. show
10. c. well
11. b. busy
12. c. just
13. a. may
14. b. a few
15. b. details

Vocabulary Self-Test 2 (Units 3–4, pages 117–118)

1. b. catch
2. c. information
3. b. if
4. c. Each
5. b. world
6. a. try
7. a. around
8. a. wrong
9. b. reports
10. c. seems
11. a. decide
12. b. own
13. c. mistakes
14. c. remember
15. c. worry
16. b. so
17. a. nothing
18. a. carry

Vocabulary Self-Test 3 (Units 1–5, pages 148–149)

1. b. facts
2. c. Let's
3. b. soon
4. a. anything
5. b. remember
6. a. half
7. b. should
8. d. angry
9. c. a few
10. a. problems
11. d. life
12. a. change
13. d. during
14. c. well
15. b. opinion
16. c. believe
17. d. too
18. a. mean
19. a. reason
20. c. expect
21. d. hard
22. b. hold
23. a. enjoys
24. c. stress
25. d. future

INDEX TO TARGET VOCABULARY

REFERENCES, ACKNOWLEDGMENTS, AND PHOTOGRAPHY CREDITS

REFERENCES

"Collecting: Collectibles for Kids." Retrieved December 2, 2008, from http://www.essortment.com/all/colectablescol_rzzv.htm.

Cuthbert, M. "The Six Basic Types of E-Shoppers." *E-Commerce Times* (September 29, 2000). Retrieved December 2, 2008, from http://www.ecommercetimes.com/story/4430.html.

Jones, M. "Collecting Pieces of Childhood." *Milwaukee Journal Sentinel* (September 8, 2002). Retrieved December 2, 2008, from http://www.lunchboxpad.com/home/information/newsbox/articles/0065.shtml.

ACKNOWLEDGMENTS

I would like to thank Mayda Saldana, Will Daniel, and Daniel Butler for sharing their stories with me for *New Password 1*. I would also like to thank my beginning reading students at Holyoke Community College (Holyoke, MA, USA), whose responses to the readings and exercises we used in class helped to shape the book.

I also very much appreciate the work of the following reviewers, who commented on early drafts of materials for the book: Simon Weedon, NOVA ICI Oita School, Japan; Joe Walther, Sookmyung Women's University, Korea; Kevin Knight, Kanda University of International Studies, Japan; Guy Elders, Turkey; Wendy Allison, Seminole Community College, Florida; Kimberly Bayer-Olthoff, Hunter College, New York; Ruth Ann Weinstein, J.E. Burke High School, Massachusetts; Vincent LoSchiavo, P.S. 163, New York; Kelly Roberts-Weibel, Edmunds Community College, Washington; Lisa Cook, Laney College, California; Thomas Leverett, Southern Illinois University, Illinois; Angela Parrino, Hunter College, New York; Adele Camus, George Mason University, Virginia.

Finally, it has been a pleasure working with Pearson Longman ELT, and for all their efforts on behalf of this book and the entire *New Password* series, I would like to thank Pietro Alongi, Editorial Director; Amy McCormick, Acquisitions Editor; Paula Van Ells, Director of Development; Thomas Ormond, Development Editor; Len Shalansky and Susan Tait Porcaro, Illustrators; Wendy Campbell and Carlos Rountree, Assistant Editors; Helen Ambrosio, Project Editor and Photo Researcher; and the rest of the Pearson Longman ELT team.

PHOTOGRAPHY CREDITS